RETURN
OF THE
TRIBAL

NEOTRIBAL FANTASY

A STRIKING EXAMPLE OF A TRULY PERSONAL TATTOO DESIGN, IN A RATHER UNUSUAL

PLACE OF THE BODY. THIS FASHIONABLE NEOTRIBAL TATTOO—THE PART IN

DARK BLUE INK—HAS BEEN ELEGANTLY ENHANCED BY THE TWO PARTS

THAT LOOK LIKE GEMSTONES INLAID INTO THE SKIN.

RETURN OF THE TRIBAL

A Celebration of Body Adornment

PIERCING • TATTOOING • SCARIFICATION • BODY PAINTING

Rufus C. Camphausen

PARK STREET PRESS

ROCHESTER, VERMONT

Park Street Press
One Park Street
Rochester, Vermont 05767
www.gotoit.com

Library of Congress Cataloging-in-Publication Data

Camphausen, Rufus C.
    Return of the tribal : a celebration of body adornment : piercing, tattooing, scarification,
body painting / Rufus C. Camphausen.
        p.   cm.
    Includes bibliographical references.
    ISBN 0-89281-610-4
    1. Body marking 2. Body piercing. 3. Tattooing.   I. Title.
    GN419.15.C35 1997   97-17043
    391.6'5—dc21   CIP

Printed and bound in Hong Kong

10 9 8 7 6 5 4 3 2 1

Text design by Bonnie Atwater
Text layout by Peri Champine
This book was typeset in Phaistos with Xavier and Metropolis as display typefaces

Park Street Press is a division of Inner Traditions International

Distributed to the book trade in Canada by Publishers Group West (PGW), Toronto, Ontario
Distributed to the book trade in the United Kingdom by Deep Books, London
Distributed to the book trade in Australia by Millennium Books, Newtown, N.S.W.
Distributed to the book trade in New Zealand by Tandem Press, Auckland
Distributed to the book trade in South Africa by Alternative Books, Ferndale

Contents

Introduction

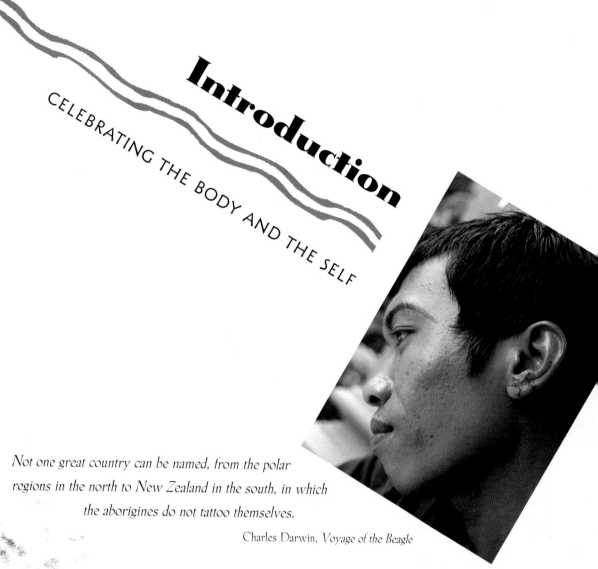

Not one great country can be named, from the polar regions in the north to New Zealand in the south, in which the aborigines do not tattoo themselves.

Charles Darwin, *Voyage of the Beagle*

And the Lord spake unto Moses, saying: Ye shall not round the corners of your heads, neither shalt thou mar the corners of thy beard. Ye shall not make any cuttings in your flesh, nor print any mark upon you: I am the Lord.

Leviticus 19:1, 27–28 (King James translation)

IN THIS BOOK I shall attempt to provide ample evidence, in text and images, that the great variety of practices aiming at adorning, beautifying, or even modifying the human body are the most ancient and most direct expression of human creativity, known and practiced all over the globe and at all times.

In recent decades, various forms of body adornment and decoration—such as makeup, ear piercing, some body painting, and much cosmetic surgery—have become more or less accepted by our contemporary societies, whereas others—nonmainstream practices such as piercing the eyebrows, lips, breasts, and genitals; decorating the skin by tattooing, scarification, or branding; or completely changing the shape and look of one's body—are often thought of as weird, strange, slightly perverted, or outright asocial.

The last years have brought an explosion of interest in—and demand for—all types of body decoration, though it is mainly tattooing, followed by piercings of all kinds, that has undergone a true renaissance. Once the domain of people at the fringe of society, tattooing (and piercing in its wake) is slowly becoming as accepted as lipstick and face-lifts. This is evidenced by popular trading cards, advertisements of major companies, and the appearance of more and more tattooed heroes and heroines on the screen and in the fashion world.

These pages will show that the impulse to shape one's body and one's self in one's own desired image, far from being something only for social outcasts, seems as intrinsic to being human as are (self)consciousness, art, communication, and sexuality.

To those with a prejudice against these practices, I would like to say that they are quite normal, once one looks at humanity as a whole rather than assuming that the conventional values held by many of our contemporaries are the only valid ones. To those who contemplate joining the new and fashionable trend by getting their first tattoo or piercing soon, I would like to show the multidimensional background of these traditions in tribal societies of the past and present.

As more and more individuals fully reclaim control over their minds and bodies—a basic human right, yet often usurped by political or religious groups—we see them revive not only such ancient arts as tattooing and piercing but also—more or less simultaneously—many other forms of self-expression within the

DRESSED TO LIVE

❈ ❈ ❈

BODY-DECORATED PEOPLE, BOTH MEN AND
WOMEN, OFTEN ADOPT A NEW DRESS CODE.
WHETHER AT PRIVATE PARTIES, IN SOME DISCOS,
OR AT THE MANY ANNUAL TATTOO CONVEN-
TIONS, THEY FIND WAYS OF DRESSING THAT DIS-
PLAY THEIR DECORATIONS MOST ADVANTA-
GEOUSLY. HARKING BACK TO THE FASHIONS OF
ANCIENT CRETE AND EGYPT, BARE BREASTS
ARE SLOWLY LEAVING THE BEACHES
AND MAKING THEIR COMEBACK
INTO CONTEMPORARY LIFE.

KARO MAN
✼ ◉ ✼

ELABORATE HAIR DESIGN, BODY
PAINTING, AND MULTIPLE PIERCINGS
OF THE EAR ARE THE TRADEMARK OF
MANY A KARO MAN OF ETHOPIA.
HOWEVER, SCARIFICATION OF THE
CHEST, OR WEARING A GRAY AND
OCHRE HAIR BUN AS THE MAN IN THIS
PHOTO DOES, IS ALLOWED ONLY TO
THOSE WHO HAVE KILLED AN ENEMY
OR A DANGEROUS ANIMAL. THE SAME
HOLDS TRUE AMONG THE KARO'S
NEIGHBORS, THE HAMAR.

TRADITION MEETS TECHNOLOGY

JUST AS DISH ANTENNAS CAN
NOW BE FOUND IN THE
DEEPEST REGIONS OF BORNEO'S
RAINFOREST, SO CAN ONE MEET
TRADITIONALLY ADORNED TRIBAL PEOPLE IN
THE MODERN CITY OF KUCHING. HOWEVER,
WHEREAS OTHER TRIBAL PEOPLE OFTEN
DISCARD THEIR HEAVY EARRINGS WHEN
LEAVING THEIR VILLAGES, THIS ORANG ULU
WOMAN PROUDLY DISPLAYS HER TRADITIONAL
JEWELRY TO THE WORLD AT LARGE.

social context. Seemingly modern forms of sexuality—especially in group-related forms—indicate that self-directed humans are more playful than the rules and regulations of the last centuries have led most of us to imagine. Again simultaneously, the last three decades have shown a return of many people to values, practices, and ways of thinking that were born in shamanic societies of old—for example, the ritual and communal use of drugs and other techniques aimed at personal transformation by way of ecstatic and extraordinary experiences.

The emergence or renaissance of the ancient tribal arts of body adornment is by no means restricted to the present generation of men and women in Western countries. After having been outlawed and suppressed by Christian or Islamic missionaries and the resulting governments for a century or two, young Samoans, Hawaiians, Maori, and others in Oceania are also reviving their ancient and traditional arts. Stimulated by the new appreciation of, and demand for, their arts and knowledge, peoples from the Pacific to Africa are now recovering and reviving what was almost lost, motivated and helped by a new kind of tourist who is interested in these practices.

Together, all these apparently unrelated "movements" clearly spell out that we are witnessing a Return to the Tribal—something that Marshall McLuhan profoundly sensed and predicted thirty years ago:

> Ours is a brand-new world of allatonceness. . . . We now live in a global village; a simultaneous happening. . . . We have begun again to structure the primordial feeling, the tribal emotions from which a few centuries of literacy divorced us.[1]

THE PENDULUM OF HISTORY: BODY ADORNMENT AND MODIFICATION IN THE FLOW OF TIME

circa 60,000 B.C.E.	Australian Aborigines, probably the oldest peoples still now surviving, practiced body painting and ritual scarification as well as penile subincision and elongation of the labia.
15–10,000 B.C.E.	Masked figures in the rock engravings of La Madeleine (Dordogne, France) show signs of body painting, possibly tattoos.

8–5000 B.C.E.	Many of the images at Tassili (Sahara) show markings that probably represent scarification or body painting.
	The Vedas, India's earliest sacred scriptures, mention the goddess Lakshmi as having her nose and earlobes pierced.
7000 B.C.E.	Skull elongation was practiced in Neolithic Jericho, one of history's first urban centers.
4200 B.C.E.	Egyptian mummies of two Nubian women show a series of tattooed lines across their abdomens.[2]
4000 B.C.E.	Men in pre-dynastic Egypt wore decorated penis sheaths, and women were tattooed.[3] Also, pharoahs and other members of the royal family are usually depicted with elongated skulls.
3000 B.C.E.	"Circum-Pacific" cultural zone, as proposed by Heine Geldern, was formed.[4] This means, in plain language, that most of the techniques practiced by peoples from Borneo to Hokkaido to Samoa to the Amazon—such as tattooing; piercing of noses, lips, ears, and genitals; and earlobe elongation—may be roughly five thousand years old.
2200 B.C.E.	A mummified priestess of the Goddess Hathor, during the eleventh dynasty in Egypt, shows tattoos.
1900 B.C.E.	Anthropomorphic figures of deities in the eastern Mediterranean cultural zone, Eastern Europe, and the Near East show markings that could be tattoos or body painting.
1500 B.C.E.	The Mesoamerican Olmec culture, and later ones influenced by it, practiced tattooing, scarification, skull elongation, and a variety of piercings, including the forehead and the genitals.
1000 B.C.E.	In Egypt and Nuba, dancers and prostitutes were tattooed on the thighs or pubic area.
500 B.C.E.	Approximate date for the archeological find, in the Altai Mountains, Siberia, of the mummified skin of a male hand, tattooed with mythical animals.

IDENTITY AND
FREEDOM

A GOLDEN RING IN THE FRONT OF
THE RIGHT NOSTRIL IS THE TRADE-
MARK OF HADENDAWA WOMEN,
WHEREAS OTHER BEJA—ALL MUSLIM
AND HEAVILY VEILED—WEAR
DIFFERENT TYPES OF NOSE-RINGS.
AS WITH OTHER TRIBES ACROSS THE
WORLD, PEOPLE'S ADORNMENTS ARE
OFTEN DETERMINED BY BEING BORN
INTO A PARTICULAR TRIBE. SUCH
RESTRAINTS DO NOT EXIST FOR
PEOPLE IN NON-TRIBAL SOCIETIES.
THE ELEGANT AND UNUSUAL TAT-
TOOS BEFITTING THE ELEGANT LADY
AT RIGHT IS A DESIGN TRULY
UNIQUE TO HERSELF.

FRESH SCARS

ONCE HEALED, THE LINES OF THIS RECENTLY CUT SCARIFICATION WILL CERTAINLY ENHANCE THE OVERALL LOOK OF THIS ALREADY BEAUTIFUL HAND.

SURI WOMAN, ETHIOPIA

IT TAKES ONLY SIX MONTHS TO STRETCH THE LIPS TO DIMENSIONS THAT CAN HOLD THE HUGE LIP-PLATES OF WOOD OR CLAY THAT ARE WORN BY SURI WOMEN. THE PLATES CAN EASILY BE TAKEN OUT FOR PRIVATE MEALS OR SLEEP. OTHERWISE, THEY MAY BE TAKEN OUT ONLY WHEN THE WEARER IS IN THE COMPANY OF OTHER WOMEN. SOME TRIBES HAVE INTRODUCED THESE PLATES AS A MEANS TO LESSEN QUARRELS WITHIN THE TRIBE; IF A PERSON CAN'T SPEAK THE WHOLE DAY, FEWER IRRITATIONS WILL ARISE IN THE COMMUNITY.

450 B.C.E.	Faces on Japanese clay figures show tattoos.[5]
	Herodotus (484–420) reports that the Thracian aristocracy wears tattoos and that leading Greek citizens were often tattooed according to their profession.
400 B.C.E.	The Maya, like various peoples in Africa, chipped their front teeth in a way that made them look like animal fangs.
250 B.C.E.	Chinese and Korean literary records show that the full-body tattoo was practiced in Japan.
200 B.C.E.	Plastic surgery documented in India: a lost nose was reconstructed with folds of skin.
	In Greece, slaves were marked by branding.
Fifth century	Roman soldiers gave the name *Picts* to Gallic warriors who went into battle naked, displaying their "fearsome" tattoos. The centurians, the reigning caesar's elite bodyguards, enhanced their show of strength and virility by displaying their pierced and bejeweled nipples.
550	In Japan, people of the lower castes (butchers, executioners, circus people, and others) were marked by tattoos on their arms.
720	In Japan, facial tattoos (for example, the word *traitor*) were used to mark delinquents, and the aristocracy was also still marked with tiny tattoos near the eye.[6]
Thirteenth century	In Japan, tattooing was no longer restricted to the lower classes and became regarded as a fine art.
1685	The "Black Code" specified that black slaves should be marked by a brand on the chest.
1791	Until this time, craftsmen throughout Europe were identified, in the absence of written diplomas, by tattoos that were proof of their profession.
Eighteenth century	Japan ended the use of tattoos or branding to mark criminals, yet tattoos remained stigmatized and only social outsiders, such as prostitutes, had them.

This century of discovery, with now-famous explorers roaming the world by sea, saw many sailors get tattooed in styles influenced by the peoples they "discovered."

In Europe, the technique of elongating a child's skull slowly ceased to be practiced. Before this time, it was known from Holland to France and eastward into the Caucasus.

Nineteenth century Having been imported from China via a kind of comic book, around 1750, the artistic full-body tattoo so characteristic of Japan reached the height of its development.[7]

1852 In France, printed police records replaced the practice of marking thieves by tattooing a fleur-de-lis on the right shoulder.

1870 In Japan, tattooing was forbidden by Emperor Meiji, and the ban remained until 1945.

1882 The Japanese art of tattooing reached Victorian England through the works of tattoo masters such as Sutherland MacDonald, whose clientele included several monarchs of this time. In the wake of this event, many Chinese and Japanese tattoo experts moved to Europe and the United States, and local artists also learned this trade.[8] This new popularity also resulted in the exhibition of tattooed people at fairgrounds.

1891 Invention of the electric tattooing machine.

1939 to 1945 In Germany, Hitler's henchmen tattooed prisoners in con-centration camps with a number on the arm. Members of the SS, however, were tattooed with their blood group in the left armpit to aid doctors in treating them.

In the wake of Hitler's proposal for an ideal race, some par-ents revived a form of skull modeling in order to make a round baby's head into a high, longish one conforming to the proposed "master race."[9]

1945	Tattooing was once again allowed in Japan.
1950s	Subcultures such as the early rockers and teddy boys helped bring the tattoo to a new popularity.[10] Also, the mohawk hairstyle, based on the practice of a Native American tribe, appeared among members of New York City street gangs.
1960s to 1980s	More subcultures, from hippies to Hell's Angels and punks, practiced tattooing extensively, often as a language of defiance against prevalent social norms. At the same time, body piercing became popular in the gay leather scene, or "tribe," of San Francisco. Specific names associated with this trend are Doug Malloy (d. 1979), Jim Ward (of Gauntlet), Fakir Musafar (of Body Play), and Alan Oversby (a.k.a. Mr. Sebastian).
1970s	Punks, apart from often wearing tattoos, also adopted such tribal techniques as piercing and coloring their hair like that of Papuan warriors, and they, too, adopted the mohawk hairstyle.
1977	Fakir Musafar coined the term *Modern Primitives* and introduced tribal and spiritual concepts and language into the growing ranks of those who practiced piercing and other forms of body modification.
1989	Publication of the book *Modern Primitives*, largely responsible for popularizing so-called neotribal tattoos as well as a further resurgence of techniques such as piercing, branding, and scarification, often performed in a more or less public and/or ritual context. England's immediate attempt to ban this book on charges of obscenity helped make it famous.[11]
1990	Musician Perry Farrell created the first so-called *Lollapalooza* tour. With Farrell himself being tattooed, scarified, and adorned with multiple piercings, and the show being a kind of wild, tribal-like gathering combining entertainment with political and human rights concerns, the tribal renaissance already in process was enhanced.

KAIAPO WARRIOR WITH LIP-PLATE AND PIPE

>>>>>>>>>>>>>>>>

ALTHOUGH MUCH OF TRADITIONAL KAIAPO CULTURE IS STILL ALIVE AND GENERAL NUDITY, BODY PAINTING, AND ELONGATION OF THE EARLOBES ARE WIDELY PRACTICED, THE CUSTOMARY LIP-PLATE OF THE MEN IS DISAPPEARING. THIS PHOTOGRAPH SHOWS IREKUM, ONE OF THE FEW MEN STILL TO WEAR SUCH A PLATE.

DARING TEENAGERS

>>>>>>>>>>>>>>

EVEN IN SMALL TOWNS AND RURAL AREAS, SUCH AS ROCHESTER, VERMONT, THE MORE DARING AND ADVENTUROUS YOUTHS HAVE BEGUN TO EXPERIMENT WITH PIERCINGS.

INITIATION AND DEATH

>>>>>>>>>>>>>

AMONG THE LOBI OF UPPER VOLTA, THE BOYS AND GIRLS TO BE INITIATED ARE PAINTED IN A MANNER THAT MAKES THEIR BODIES RESEMBLE SKELETONS. OUR OWN ASSOCIATION OF A SKELETON WITH DEATH, MERELY A CULTURAL BIAS, DOES NOT ACTUALLY BEAR ON THIS. RATHER, AMONG TRIBAL PEOPLES IN AFRICA, AUSTRALIA, AND PAPUA NEW GUINEA, SUCH SKELETON PAINTINGS INDICATE THEIR SENSORY ABILITY OF "X-RAY VISION," WHICH IS COMPARABLE TO THE SONIC ABILITY OF DOLPHINS TO DETECT CHANGES AND DISEASES IN SOMEONE ELSE'S BODY. SEE PAGE 53 FOR A CROSS-CULTURAL EXAMPLE.

1980s to 1990s   More and more research on tribal people, their arts, and lifestyles, and more and more available images of body-decorated people have led to the publication of many specialized books and magazines (see Bibliography).

Unfortunately, many techniques and many peoples do not appear in this short history of adornment and modification, simply because certain techniques have no known chronicle. In India, for example, piercing and tattooing have long been part of the tradition, yet there is no record of when these practices started. Similarly, in the absence of a written history, we cannot know when people from the African deserts to the Amazon rainforest truly began painting their bodies or elongating their earlobes and lips. To say they have done so since the beginning of time does not help. Yet, I am convinced—as an avid student of history and anthropology—that most of these practices are older than any existing and archeologically validated works of art, which started to appear about 30,000 years ago. One must not forget that, with the exception of mummies, all art on the human body disappears into fire or ashes along with its bearer. The arts of body decoration and modification are truly ephemeral.

1

Skin and Bone, Body and Soul

ANCIENT AND MODERN PRACTICES OF BODY ADORNMENT

SINCE THE DAWN of humanity, a great variety of practices and techniques have been employed by both sexes to decorate, beautify, enhance, and modify the body we inherit at birth. The practices range from full-body painting; facial makeup; tattoos; and wearing jewelry, lingerie, and clothes to the piercing of ears, noses, mouths, and nipples; genital adornment and enhancement; shaving, cutting, or coloring of one's hair; and more permanent modifications through sacrification, amputation, binding, or elongation.

Whereas many people today who decorate their bodies are motivated mainly by a personal or collective rebellion against a culture that seems to reduce humans to mere numbers, or by fashions inspired by the streets and the media, tribal cultures have a great variety of other motivations for these practices. Some decorations are self-motivated expressions of personal freedom and uniqueness. Most, however, have to do with traditions that mark the person as a member or nonmember of the local group, or express religious, magical, or spiritual beliefs and convictions.

In most parts of the world, tribal people have used body decoration for a variety of reasons:

- to indicate one's affiliation to a clan, tribe, or totemic group
- to indicate one's age group, social ranking, or status
- to mark slaves and/or criminals
- as a sign of mourning
- to deflect evil and illness
- to gain entry, on dying, into the other world
- to attain magical powers
- to appear fierce and frightening to enemies
- to be (more) attractive to others and/or oneself
- to enhance sexual stimulation for oneself and/or one's partner(s)

Seen from an individual point of view, or from within the framework of a given group, society, or culture, certain of these practices are regarded as normal or harmless. But whoever moves beyond the currently accepted behavior or defined boundaries is usually labeled with terms that range from crazy or weird to criminal or pathological. It is important to remember that other people's cultural and spirtual practices are no less valid than our own.

Numerous practices of body adornment and modification range from Cain's mark in the Old Testament and Maori facial tattoos to the piercing, branding, and scarification of contemporary urban tribals in London, New York, Tokyo, and Amsterdam and neotribals throughout the world. If we look at the variety of these body adornment techniques with a more or less impartial eye, it is evident that in all these different practices—ranging from shaving and from applying eyeliner to amputating the foreskin—only a few similarities can be discerned. The clearest patterns emerge when

NUBA PERSONAL ART

UNLIKE THE MANY OTHER PEO-
PLES WHO OFTEN USE BODY
PAINTING AND OTHER MARKS TO
SYMBOLIZE AN INDIVIDUAL'S AGE
OR STATUS, PEOPLE IN SOUTHEAST
NUBA HAVE A GREAT DEGREE OF
CREATIVE FREEDOM IN THEIR
DESIGNS, WITHIN A FEW LIMITS
IMPOSED BY TRADITION. MOST
NUBA BODY ART, LIKE THAT
SHOWN HERE, FURTHER DISTIN-
GUISHES ITSELF BY A GREAT DEAL
OF ATTENTION TO SYMMETRY OR
ASYMMETRY. NOTICE ALSO THE
PIERCED UPPER LEFT EAR.

SUN GODDESS

EVEN MORE DETAIL AND MORE CREATIVE
FREEDOM THAN IN THE NUBA EXAMPLE
ABOVE HAS LED TO THE BEAUTIFUL
EXAMPLE OF CONTEMPORARY BODY
PAINTING AT LEFT. ARTIST NATASHA VON
ROSENSCHILDE SPECIALIZES IN USING THE
SKIN OF BEAUTIFUL WOMEN AND MEN AS
HER CANVAS, THUS CREATING STUNNING
IMAGES THAT TURN THESE PEOPLE INTO
COSMIC ARCHETYPES. SEE PAGES 25, 36 AND
50 FOR MORE OF HER WORK.

we use the objective criteria of permanence (how long the decoration lasts) and possible structural change to the body (whether it is soft tissue or bone that is altered) rather than arbitrary cultural standards. Thus, using the available evidence presented by ancient and modern practices, we can classify the great variety of techniques of decorating, enhancing, and modifying the human body into a simple fourfold scheme: noninvasive, invasive,* temporary, and/or permanent.

NONINVASIVE PRACTICES

Noninvasive practices include all methods of body decoration that are applied only to the body's surface. Noninvasive techniques do not involve any structural change or modification of the body or any of its parts; they remain superficial in the true sense of the word. Typical examples of noninvasive body decoration range from using nail polish to wearing clip-on earrings, from changing the color of one's hair to wearing colored contact lenses, and from facial makeup to full-fledged body painting, coloring of teeth, face design, foot design, hand design, and growing long fingernails.

INVASIVE PRACTICES

This classification refers to those techniques that modify any part of the body—temporarily or permanently—by means of elongating, perforating, cutting, or amputating; introducing foreign substances; or changing the body's bone structure. Typical examples of invasive body decoration range from specialized haircuts, "permanent makeup," piercing, and tattooing to the elongation of the neck or skull, circumcision, subincision, and cliterodectomy.

Invasive body decorations:
- *Temporary:* cosmetic tattoo, simple piercing
- *Permanent modifications:* beading, elongation of earlobes, elongation of labia,

---

*Although the term *invasive* has a slightly negative connotation, I do not imply any such negativity by using it. *Invasive,* in this context, simply indicates that skin or other tissue is "invaded" by a tool and/or material. Rather than creating a new term without negative connotations, I have preferred to use this one, which is used by many scientific publications.

certain types of cosmetic surgery, infibulation, insertion of ear-disks, insertion of lip-plugs, enlargement of piercings, scarification (branding and cutting), subincision, tattoo

- *Permanent modifications involving bone:* certain types of cosmetic surgery, elongation of the skull, elongation of the neck, foot-binding
- *Amputations:* castration, circumcision, clitoridectomy, certain types of cosmetic surgery, finger sacrifice, labial removal, tooth extraction, tooth filing

TEMPORARY DECORATIONS

To the temporary decorations belong all those techniques that *seem* to change the body but in fact only change its surface appearance and possibly the individual's sense of self and personality. Temporary decorations can be classified as either short term or long term, depending on the length of time they endure once they have been applied.

A typical short-term decoration is noninvasive and can be fully removed at any given time after its application. Depending on the materials used, these decorations may disappear fully or they may leave traces for a short while. Typical examples of short-term decorations are facial makeup, hair removal, coloring of teeth, and body painting.

A long-term decoration cannot easily be removed because of the invasive nature, however slight, of its application to the body. The only natural manner of removal is in the form of the regenerative powers of the body over time. A typical example of long-term decoration is the contemporary cosmetic tattoo, also known as "permanent makeup," which lasts about three to six years. Another is the decoration applied to the hands or feet with henna dye. Piercing can be a temporary adornment, given that a simple perforation of the skin will often close again once the inserted jewelry is taken out for a length of time, though for our purposes we will classify piercing as a permanent change.

PERMANENT CHANGES

Most types of body decorations that are permanent are invasive modifications, with piercing and scarification as the foremost examples. Permanent modifications come in several distinct types, depending on whether only soft tissue (skin or flesh)

MODERN VIKING

ALTHOUGH FACIAL TATTOS CAN PROVE TROUBLESOME WITHIN SOCIETIES WHERE SUCH TRADITION DOES NOT EXIST, THE YOUNG GERMAN SHOWN HERE HAS FOUND OUT THAT PEOPLE DO GET USED TO HIS MULTIPLE TATTOS ONCE THEY KNOW HIM, AND THAT PREJUDICE THEN USUALLY DISAPPEARS WITH TIME.

INDIAN PILGRIM

UNIQUE, HEAVY GOLDEN JEWELRY IS WORN BY THIS AGED INDIAN WOMAN IN HER PIERCED EARS, NOSTRILS, AND NASAL SEPTUM. ONE SHOULD REALIZE THAT THIS WOMAN IS NOT "TRIBAL" BUT—WITHIN HER CULTURE—A TRUE CONTEMPORARY. DURING HER PILGRIMAGES, SHE SHAVED HER HAIR IN ORDER TO OFFER IT TO HER DEITY.

EAR INSERTS

TURKANA WOMAN FROM KENYA
WITH MULTIPLE PIERCINGS ALONG
THE OUTSIDE EDGE OF HER EAR.

HENNA DYE

THE HAND OF THIS SWAHILI
WOMAN FROM LAMU, KENYA,
SHOWS THAT HENNA PASTE CAN BE
USED TO COLOR THE FINGERNAILS
AND TO CREATE INTRICATE DESIGNS
ON THE SKIN.

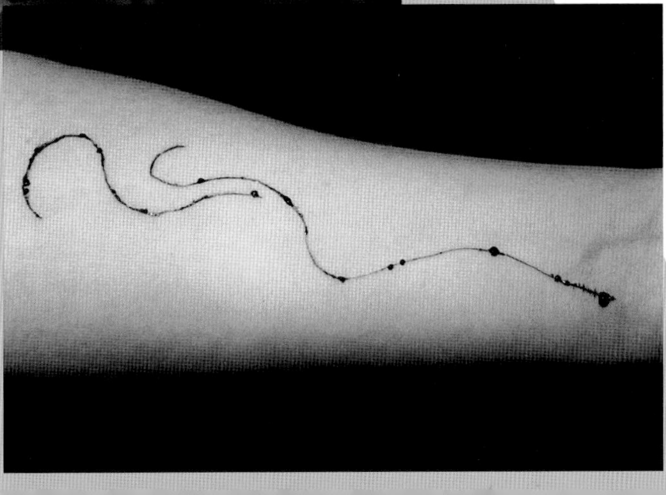

CONTEMPORARY SCARIFICATION

PHOTOGRAPHED SHORTLY
AFTER THE INCISIONS HAVE BEEN
MADE, THESE STILL-BLOODY
SCARS WILL SOON TURN INTO A
SOFT AND FLOWING DESIGN, LESS
VISIBLE THAN A TATTOO BUT
COMMEMORATING FOR ALL
TIMES THE EFFORT OF WILL THAT
WAS NEEDED TO ENDURE AND
TRANSFORM THE PAIN
ACCOMPANYING THE CUTTING.

is involved or whether the body's bone structure is actually altered.

Soft-tissue alterations include tattoos, circumcision, and face-lifts as well as piercings that are enlarged and kept open over time (for example, with disks, plugs, or sticks inserted in the ears or lips).

Soft-tissue alterations:
- *Decorations:* cosmetic tattoo, simple piercings that are not enlarged
- *Modifications:* certain types of cosmetic surgery, elongation of earlobes, elongation of labia, infibulation, insertion of ear-disks, insertion of lip-plugs, enlarged piercings, scarification (branding and cutting), subincision, tattoo
- *Amputations:* castration, circumcision, clitoridectomy, removal of labia

Hard-tissue changes, or structural changes to bones, occur in such practices as elongation of the skull or neck, filing the teeth, or inlaying the teeth with precious stones. All of these changes are invasive, permanent modifications. Some of these practices are actual amputations that result in the permanent loss of a part of the body, however small.

Hard-tissue alterations:
- *Bone changes:* elongation oof the skull, elongation of the neck, foot-binding
- *Amputation:* finger sacrifice, tooth extraction, tooth filing, certain types of cosmetic surgery

Many of these practices have surfaced over the last few decades in the urban centers of both Eastern and Western societies. But they differ in several ways from those that are and have been practiced by tribal peoples across the globe. Whereas, for example, tattooing and piercing various parts of the body are more or less common in many cultures and across time, some practices have not yet resurfaced here and may never do so. Elongation of the skull, for example, as has been practiced in China and Egypt, or elongation of the neck, as is still done in Burma, do not occur in our societies. These are techniques that have to be set in motion at a very early age, and parents who would attempt to do so today would almost certainly end up in prison.

In societies such as ours, where the body is usually covered, body-decorated men and women often feel the need to adopt a new dress code in order to show or exhibit the artistic creations that have become part of their bodies and selves. Whether at private parties, in some discos, or at the many annual tattoo conventions, ways of dressing are found that display these decorations most advantageously (see page 3). Harking back to the fashions of ancient Crete and Egypt, bare breasts are slowly leaving the beaches and making their comeback into urban life.

Certain individuals, however, seem to go too far for almost everyone's taste but their own. Sometimes, especially within the "inner circle" of those who have acquired multiple tattoos and piercings, the old human spirit of competition comes forward. In those cases, it seems that all moderation is lost and the question becomes merely: Who has the most? Who dares the most? Who is most outrageous?

With all due respect for people's individual choices and all celebrations of one's body, I believe there are certain borders it is better not to cross in order to remain an accepted member of whatever group, and certain practices it is better not to follow or encourage, such as forced clitoridectomy, circumcision, or castration. Those latter practices do not result in the dazzling works of art produced by men and women of the world's remaining tribal cultures, which seem to compete with the spectacular, colorful, and exotic plants, birds, and butterflies that are part of their environment, nor do they result in the joy that is visibly expressed between the young flirting Ethiopian couple on page 72.

Whether one applies simple facial makeup, full-body painting, multiple scarifications, tattoos, or piercings, it is my conviction that only those adornments, decorations, and modifications that enhance joy in living and a person's love and respect for self and others are true expressions of humanity. All such enhancements, whether temporary or permanent, invasive or not, are expressions of celebrating the body, celebrating the self, and celebrating life as a human being.

I Am Marked, Therefore I Am

THE SELF IN THE SOCIAL MIRROR

LIKE IT OR NOT, none of us can escape being reflected in the mirror that consists of the eyes—and thoughts—of all others we encounter in a given moment and throughout our lives. We may feel or act as individuals as much as we like, need, or dare; yet we still cannot escape the fact that we are members of small and large groups—family or tribe, society or subculture, clan or totem, gender or race. If all else fails, each of us is at least a member of humanity, that particular species of primates known for a few essential traits that differentiate it from all others.

One of these human traits, although schoolteachers around the world forget to mention it when they speak about brains, intelligence, and verbal and manual skills, is the love and need for adornment, decoration, and true modification of the human body.

Almost all peoples of all ages and all continents have done so—and continue to do so—and for a variety of reasons and with various motivations. Specific ways of body adornment and modification have been and are applied with completely different rationales. From the point of view of a group, they have been applied in order to mark someone as a member of the general group but also in order to mark someone as not being a member, as an outcast: the famous Biblical mark of Cain. From the point of view of the individual, again, one can mark oneself as a member and/or one can try to present or exaggerate oneself as an individual not bound by the dictates of others.

The combination of these four related yet different motivations has led to a particularly rich art form, which only recently has become recognized as such. It has also led to a rich history of approval and disapproval, sanction, or prohibition. Primarily, it has led to a great virtual library of signs, symbols, and techniques, and today, in the age of information distribution, we can, as many do, draw on all that our ancestors all over the world have done. Sometimes ancient techniques and symbols are faithfully copied; at other times they are adapted more or less skillfully and changed more or less successfully.

The two most basic distinctions of marks seem to be whether or not we are dealing with a *mark of Cain* or with a *mark of civi-lization.** The clearly negative mark of Cain was used in many cul-tures, from Canaan of the Old Testament to modern Japan, and from ancient China to twentieth-century Nazi Germany. In such cases, the tattoo or another way of marking the skin has been used to mark murderers and other criminals and also to brand human slaves in the manner of cattle. A similar practice has also been used by tribal peoples, for example, to publicly shame someone for cowardice. In that manner, a former chief of the Dayaks in Borneo was marked by a large tattoo for having fled from the enemy when he should have stood with his braves.

---

* For the phrase "marks of civilization," we are indebted to resaercher Arnold Rubin, who used it as a title for his outstanding work (see Bibliography).

IBAN MAN

THIS MAN HAS THE BODY
TATTOOS TYPICAL OF
MOST OF THE DAYAK
GROUPS IN BORNEO.

SURI BODY PAINTING

A YOUNG SURI WOMAN OF ETHIOPIA
WITH SCARIFICATIONS AND LARGE EAR-
PLUGS IS BEING PAINTED. MOST OFTEN,
THIS IS DONE BY MEN OF THE TRIBE.

To the present-day sensitivities of many of us, such practices belong in the category of what we now call human rights violations. It is much easier, then, to accept one or more of those practices of marking that are intended as adornments, even though they may be as painful as being branded as a slave. On the whole, people are much more attracted to the marks of civilization: those types of tattoos or scarifications that show the individual to be a member of the group, to be initiated, or to be of a certain age or standing. These kinds of marks, adornments, and modifications have been used around the world not to set a person apart but to make that person recognizable as part of the group—someone who can be trusted or is even to be regarded as a human being at all.

Whether by requiring a full-body tattoo or by circumcising, many cultures and peoples regard only those with the right markings as pure, clean, or valuable members. Sometimes a marked member of the group is called "cooked" (seasoned, experienced, human), whereas an unmarked outsider is regarded as "raw" (an unknown and unproven entity, closer to the animals than to humans).[12]

However, in most of these cases, the individual has no real choice in the matter, neither in choosing whether to be marked at all nor concerning the time, manner, and design of marking. Most often, tribal people adhere in these matters to rather rigid traditions, into which changes creep only slowly.

Among many African peoples, for example, not only do young girls have to undergo the fearsome clitoridectomy, but the life cycle of a woman is repeatedly inscribed in painful markings on her skin. From menarche and marriage to motherhood and menopause, she is marked by painful scarifications. Less painful, but nevertheless involuntary, is the manner in which Dinka men and others paint their bodies or the way Burmese women reshape their legs with heavy metal rings.

Although most of the markings hitherto mentioned are permanent, we should realize that ephemeral forms such as the headdress of a Cherokee woman and the finery of an Afar bride equally mark their status, as does the bowler hat of an English member of Parliament or the designer clothes of a wealthy lady. In that way, most of us—usually without realizing it—have never left the customary procedures of our tribal ancestors; we merely exchanged the old codes for new ones.

Today's renewed interest in the more extreme forms of body decoration, such as punk hair styles, full-body tattoos, and facial piercings, has its very roots in

AMONG THE DINKA OF SUDAN, CLAN IDENTIFICATION MARKS ARE ACHIEVED BY PAINFUL YET ELEGANT FACIAL SCARIFICATION.

CHEROKEE WOMAN

THE ELABORATE HEADDRESS AND LARGE, HEAVY EARRINGS OF THIS CHEROKEE WOMAN (FAR LEFT) NOT ONLY MARK HER STATUS, BUT IDENTIFY HER TRIBE.

MUSLIM AFAR BRIDE

A STUNNING EXAMPLE OF CROSS-CULTURAL FERTILIZATION, THIS AFAR BRIDE FROM THE DJIBOUTI REPUBLIC SHOWS THE INFLUENCE OF INDIAN CULTURE ON PRACTICES IN AFRICA, BOTH IN THE STYLE OF DRESS AND JEWELRY AS WELL AS IN THIS PARTICULAR FORM OF NOSE PIERCING.

A MAN OF MEN

A GIANT DINKA MAN IN HIS MOST
TYPICAL STYLE OF ADORNMENT: COV-
ERED IN ASHES. WHEREAS STRANGERS
HAVE GIVEN THESE PEOPLE THE NAME
"GHOSTLY GIANTS," THE DINKA SEE
THEMSELVES AS "MONYJANG," A TERM
THAT MEANS "MEN OF MEN."

YOUNG NUBA WOMAN

THIS GIRL RECEIVED THE TRADITIONAL
SCARS WITH THE ONSET OF PUBERTY.

AFRICAN SCARIFICATION

THIS KALERI WOMAN OF NIGERIA HAS RECEIVED VARIOUS SETS OF SCARIFICATION MARKS ON HER BELLY, A PROCESS THAT BEGINS WHEN A GIRL REACHES MENARCHE.

YOUNG KALERI WOMAN, NIGERIA

A YOUNG KALERI WOMAN WITH HER FIRST SET OF SCARIFICATIONS. AS SHE IS NOT A MOTHER YET, HER MARKINGS ARE DIFFERENT FROM THE WOMAN ABOVE. UNFORTUNATELY, THIS PARTICULAR TRIBE OF BEAUTIFUL PEOPLE IS NOW ALMOST EXTINCT, BUT SIMILAR CUSTOMS OF SCARIFICATION CONTINUE IN OTHER COMMUNITIES AND REGIONS OF THE AFRICAN CONTINENT.

A NEW TATTOO

A PERFECTLY EXECUTED NEOTRIBAL DESIGN BY TATTOO ARTIST VYVYN LAZONGA, PHOTOGRAPHED IMMEDIATELY FOLLOWING THE TATTOOING.

KAYAH LADY

AMONG THE KAYAH, A BURMESE HILL-TRIBE NOW TAKING REFUGEE IN NEIGHBORING THAILAND, THE WOMEN WEAR HEAVY EARRINGS ELONGATING THEIR LOBES CONSIDERABLY.

KAYAW WOMEN OF BURMA

ALTHOUGH THE HEAVY METAL RINGS SEEM NOT TO HINDER EVERYDAY MOVEMENT, THEY COMPLETELY RESHAPE THE WOMEN'S LEGS.

those old customs, but with a changed perspective. Then, society marked the outsider to set him or her apart. Now, the real or would-be outsider marks himself or herself as a sign and proof of being a rebel, of not conforming to the standardized supermarket humanity promoted by mainstream media and society at large.

Individual choice is what makes today's renaissance of tribal practices a totally different matter. Although clearly inspired by the great variety of adornment, decoration, and modification from Africa, Asia, Oceania, and the Americas, most of today's practitioners have the added benefit of total choice as to what, where, and when they will apply their markings. Exceptions to this general rule are found in close-knit urban groups such as street gangs, where again, certain clearly defined markings are mandatory and serve as both ritual initiation and a way of establishing identity. In this way, such marks are more truly tribal than most others.

These days, anyone else who gets tattooed with tribal or neotribal designs, who pierces his or her face like a warrior, or who enlarges an earlobe in the manner of tribal people around the world, does not, without other efforts, become tribal in his or her consciousness or lifestyle. Whether or not one likes these particular techniques, the appearance of the results, or the abundance of markings that almost seem to hint at a form of addiction to a different kind of needle is not important. What is important is that each of us is allowed to choose what he or she does with body and self, just as a Padang girl (page 90) is allowed to choose whether or not to wear her neck-rings. Once chosen, however, she must do so for the rest of her life—a fact that is also true for all forms of tattooing. That dimension of freedom, and that only, is the hallmark of civilization. Let us all hope that the pendulum of permissiveness and liberty does not swing back as it has done so often in history.

By now, of course, so many "outsiders" and "rebels" have marked themselves in one or another of these ways that they have suddenly become almost mainstream themselves. Some people seem to have gotten involved in a progressive spiral of being the most outrageous of all. Once a single facial piercing, on lip or eyebrow, was enough to catch everyone's attention and the admiration of some. Now we can read of more and more brandings, scarifications, and such extreme forms as metal nails and plates inserted into the lips and even horns into the skull. To some of these extremists, neither the enhancement of beauty nor learning to deal with pain seems important; rather it's being radical that is the point.

JEN HAS IT ALL

THOSE WHO HAVE FOLLOWED THE DEVELOPMENT OF BODY ADORNMENT AND MODIFICATION IN RECENT YEARS HAVE BEEN ABLE TO NOTICE THIS WOMAN CHANGE. OFTEN PHOTOGRAPHED FOR PUBLICATION, JEN HAS HAD MORE AND MORE PIERCINGS AND TATTOOS ADDED TO HER SKIN, MAKING HERSELF INTO AN EXAMPLE OF ALMOST ALL THAT CAN BE DONE.

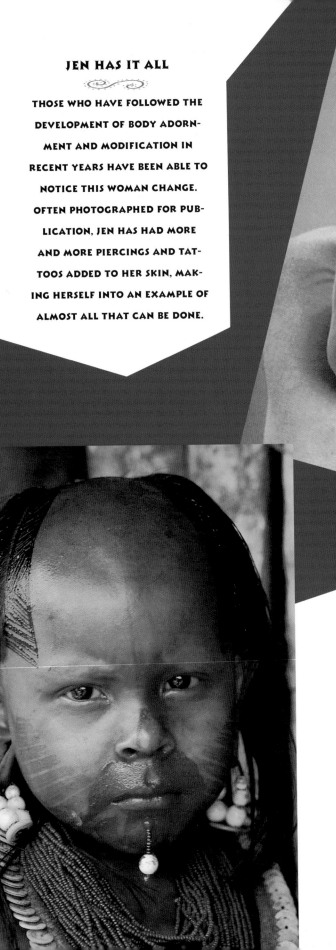

KAIAPO BOY
FROM
MEKRANOTI VILLAGE

MEKRANOTI MEANS "PEOPLE WITH BIG RED PAINT IN THEIR FACES." HOWEVER, RED PAINT IS BY NO MEANS THE ONLY MAJOR ADORNMENT OF THE KAIAPO OF CENTRAL BRAZIL. BOTH MEN AND WOMEN SHAVE THEIR HAIR IN THE PARTICULAR STYLE SHOWN HERE, USE BLACK PAINT FOR INTRICATE DESIGNS ON FACE AND BODY, AND PIERCE AND ELONGATE THEIR EARLOBES. IN THE PAST, THIS BOY'S PIERCED LOWER LIP WOULD HAVE BEEN THE FIRST STEP TOWARD THE LIP-PLUG TYPICALLY WORN BY ADULT MEN.

MIRROR, MIRROR ON THE WALL

WHO IS THE MOST INCREDIBLE OF THEM ALL? SOMETIMES THE OLD HUMAN SPIRIT OF COMPETITION SEEMS TO RULE AMONG THOSE WHO HAVE ACQUIRED MULTIPLE TATTOOS AND PIERCINGS, JUST AS IT DOES IN OTHER GROUPS AND AREAS OF LIFE.

THE FIERCE GENTLEMAN

OBVIOUSLY A WARM AND GENTLE MAN (JUST LOOK AT HIS EYES) THIS MAN FROM NEW GUINEA HAS DECORATED HIMSELF BY INSERTING THE HORNS OF A SCARAB BEETLE INTO HIS PIERCED NOSE TO LOOK LIKE A FIERCE WARRIOR OF HIS TRIBE.

3

In One's Own Image

PAINTING TO PIERCING TO TRANSFORMATION

WHEREAS THE GREAT monotheistic religions have fostered the belief that humans are made in the image of a Heavenly father-figure and have to live according to the scripts in "His book," the time has obviously arrived when a growing number of people consider this to be not only a myth but also a counterproductive one in terms of living a joyous and fulfilled life. Rather—and this is what we see emerging today concerning many issues—more and more people write their very own scripts and try to live accordingly.

The most extreme examples of this trend to (re-)create oneself in one's own image are people who spend a large part of their lives and great amounts of money to change their appearance partly or fully, by means of cosmetic surgery. Michael Jackson and his creation of an androgynous self is a well-publicized example, as is

Cindy Jackson and the Barbie-doll inspired remake of herself.*

We may not understand their motives, we may not share their extremism, and we may not agree with the fact that one's outer appearance, one's so-called beauty, should count that heavily. However, these attempts at determining not only one's own life but the look and feel of one's very flesh and bones is merely a legitimate extension of the individual freedom we all value so much. In principle, there is no difference between determining whether or not to live the heterosexual or monogamous lives prescribed by convention and deciding for ourselves how to look and when to die. The freedom to choose what to do with one's own body and life, even if that choice may be possibly harmful, is to be favored above any arbitrarily sanctioned forms of sexual behavior and/or adornment. Naturally, all of these principles are to be understood within the setting of not harming others and of mutual consent.

A look at human societies, past and present, makes it obvious that whatever is sanctioned in a given group is very, very arbitrary. One society will see as (self-)mutilation (for example, penile subincision among Australian Aborigines) what another society regards as necessary to the well-being of the group (the Aborigine's attempt to have a virtual vulva in addition to the phallus); also, practices that one may easily judge to be harmful may not at all have that effect. A good example is the ancient custom of skull elongation as it was practiced from Egypt to China, and as it is still practiced among the Mangbetu people of Zaire. There are no reports of impairment, disease, or early death among people who have such carefully and skillfully remodeled heads. Equally interesting is the custom of tooth-filing, a very painful experience that

---

*Cindy Jackson of Fremont, Ohio, had twenty-six sessions of cosmetic surgery (at a cost of more than $100,000) that changed her body into that of a "live" Barbie doll. See Bibliography for information about video tapes of this transformation.

also results in an appearance that is not very enticing. However, though we may judge this practice to be harmful, research has shown that people of African tribes who file their teeth are less suspect to a variety of diseases than others. It should be borne in mind that tribal people did not, and often do not even today, have the kind of dental care and health care that most of us have become accustomed to.

Although I have seen an image of a contemporary male Caucasian with a subincised phallus, not in print but on the Internet,[13] some tribal practices have not yet reemerged. Skull elongation is one, and the neck elongation of the Burmese Padang is another. It is interesting that in the latter case it is not, as the term implies, that the neck is elongated, but simply that the shoulders sink as their bones adapt in early childhood to the weight of the rings. The practice is, as I found out when visiting these beautiful ladies, essentially voluntarily, and most of these Burmese women do not choose to wear the rings anymore. However, the fact that many of them are now homeless refugees does entice many to choose the rings. A steady flow of tourists armed with cameras, dollars, and yen helps the women and their families survive and, last but not least, helps them finance the resistance movement in present-day Myanmar.

The return of the tribal elements into modern Western culture is present in the simpler, less painful, and less time-consuming forms of adornment such as temporary facial and body painting and, of course, in the form of piercing, a practice that has recently gained much popularity. It is interesting to see that tribal piercings are almost exclusively centered on ears, noses, and lips, often with the intent to elongate lips or lobes. Contemporary piercings are also found on foreheads and eyebrows and in the erotic and sexual regions such as the nipples, navel, and genitals (see chapter 5). Considering this, it seems that most of those pierced today, as well as many a professional piercer, have forgotten that tribal people have reasons for piercings and wearing jewelry beyond the obvious desire for adornment. As in the Chinese system of acupuncture, India's Ayurveda, for example, makes use of the marma points, and piercings were and are placed accordingly; each known and meant to stimulate or enhance specific psychosomatic processes and/or states.

An example of just how such ancient and esoteric knowledge has been used is the nostril piercing so often seen on women in India and the neighboring countries

INNER SPACE— OUTER SPACE

>>>>>>>>>>>>

CLAIREY, THE FIERCE PAINTED AND PIERCED WOMAN IN THIS PIC-TURE, HAS GIVEN OUT THE WORD THAT SHE IS AN EXTRA-TERRESTRIAL FROM VENUS. BODY DECORATION, COMBINED WITH THE RIGHT ATTIRE, CAN MAKE ANYONE INTO THE CREATURE OF HIS OR HER DREAMS, VENUSIAN OR OTHERWISE.

DENTAL FILING INSTEAD OF FILLING

<<<<<<<<<<<<

WITH PAIN STILL VISIBLE ALL OVER HIS FACE, THIS BOY FROM CENTRAL AFRICA SHOWS OFF HIS NEWLY FILED TEETH. USUALLY DESCRIBED AS AND BELIEVED TO BE A TYPE OF COSMETIC SURGERY TO ENHANCE ONE'S BEAUTY, RESEARCHERS HAVE NOW ESTABLISHED THAT PEOPLE WITH FILED TEETH—AND IN THE ABSENCE OF MODERN DENTAL CARE—ARE LESS PRONE TO A NUMBER OF DISEASES. THE FILING OF TEETH OCCURS AMONG MANY PEOPLES AROUND THE GLOBE.

SKULL ELONGATION

●━●━●━●━●

THE ANCIENT HUMAN PRACTICE OF SHAPING THE CRANIUM SO AS TO CREATE AN ELONGATED SKULL SLANTING BACK AND UPWARD HAS SURVIVED INTO THE TWENTIETH CENTURY AMONG THE UPPER-CLASS MANGBETU OF NORTHERN ZAIRE (SEE BELOW). SKULL-SHAPING IS POSSIBLE ONLY DURING THE FIRST HALF YEAR AFTER BIRTH WHEN THE SKULL BONES ARE STILL SOFT. ALTHOUGH OTHER TECHNIQUES ARE KNOWN, THE MANGBETU SIMPLY WRAP THE CHILD'S HEAD TIGHTLY WITH THICK CLOTH, CREATING A KIND OF TIGHTLY FITTING HEADGEAR THAT SHAPES THE SKULL.

IWAM WARRIOR

●━●━●━●━●

THIS MAN FROM THE UPPER SEPIK RIVER, NEW GUINEA, HAS A PIERCED NASAL SEPTUM.

of Nepal, Pakistan, and Bangladesh (see page 43). In the guise of a simple beauty enhancement—a delicate golden ring or another piece of jewelry—this piercing is actually known to help induce a state of submissiveness in the wearer. For this very reason, many women who have become aware of this and have achieved a certain degree of self-determination, even in India, now decline to have this piercing done. It can be seen in this example that the mere copying of an adornment is rarely wise. It is somewhat paradoxical that just as Indian women are discontinuing the practice, many young Western women have unknowingly put themselves in this state of mind, which—if they were aware of it—only a few would actually enjoy or choose.

Little can be said here about the limitless variety of makeup used for facial skin, eyes, eyelashes, lips, and fingernails—the cosmetics industry is most diligent in exhibiting their creations and informing us of their possibilities. Unfortunately, however, present fashions, customs, and gender-typing in most Western and Westernized societies have limited the use of makeup almost exclusively to women's faces, fingernails, and toenails. Only a few men dare, at the risk of being declared effeminate or homosexual, to break through this barrier and sometimes use a bit of makeup, just as fewer men than women wear more than a single piece of jewelry.

This was, and still is, quite different in many tribal societies. The Woodabe men of Niger and also the men of Papua New Guinea spend hours in applying makeup and making themselves look special and beautiful. When one looks at images of people from across the globe, it becomes clear that our very definition of makeup is very limited and that somehow, somewhere along the line, the border between makeup and body painting is very fluid. This can be seen by the succession of images on pages 43–46 and 49–54.

Makeup, or should we say facial design, can also be used in such a fashion as to create a virtual mask, thus consciously obliterating personal identity for a given time—for example, during a ceremony. Such a temporary loss of identity, a practice known to humanity since the earliest times, has begun to reemerge into contemporary life. From Woodstock to Lollapalooza, from house parties to "darkroom" activities, being masked—painted or otherwise—helps loosen the restraints of the

COSMIC RESONANCE

❀ ❀ ❀

HAVING INSCRIBED SUN, MOON, CLOUDS, AND STARS ONTO HER SKIN, THIS CONTEMPORARY WICCAN CAN THUS MORE EASILY ATTUNE HERSELF TO THE FORCES OF THE UNIVERSE.

PROTECTION FROM EVIL

❀ ❀ ❀

WHILE MOST PEOPLE CONSIDER THIS INDIAN GIRL'S PIERCED NOSE A SIMPLE BEAUTY ENHANCEMENT, IN ACTUALITY THIS PIERCING CREATES A STATE OF SUBMISSIVE- NESS IN THE WEARER. FORTUNATELY HER CHIN TATTOOS ARE DESIGNED TO PROTECT HER FROM HARM.

WOODABE MAN

AMONG THE WOODABE OF NIGER, IT IS CLEARLY THE MEN WHO ARE MOST GIVEN TO THE CULT OF BEAUTY AND WHO ARE, IN MODERN TERMS, THE OBJECTS OF SEXUAL ATTENTION. DURING ANNUAL FESTIVALS, THE MEN DRESS IN THEIR BEST FINERY, PUT ON THEIR BEST MAKEUP, AND TRY TO PRESENT AS MUCH OF THE WHITES OF THEIR TEETH AND EYES AS THEY CAN. AFTER THE DANCE OR PRESENTATION, WOMEN THEN WILL PICK OUT THE MEN THEY FIND MOST ATTRACTIVE.

LIP STICKS

AMONG THE YANOMAMI OF THE AMAZON, WOMEN AND CHILDREN OFTEN PIERCE THEIR LIPS, EARS, AND NOSES. INTO THE OPENINGS THUS CREATED, THEY SUBSEQUENTLY INSERT STICKS IN THE LOWER LIP, FEATHERS IN THE EAR, AND CORDS IN THE NASAL SEPTUM. SIMILAR DECORATIONS ARE KNOWN AMONG OTHER AMAZON PEOPLES, AND ALSO IN AFRICA. SUCH FACIAL AND BODY DESIGNS ARE OFTEN USED TO TRANSMIT MORE OR LESS VEILED MESSAGES BETWEEN COURTING COUPLES OR LOVERS.

FULL-FACIAL MAKEUP

RATHER THAN APPLYING A BIT OF ROUGE AND A BIT OF LIPSTICK, WOMEN FROM PAPUA NEW GUINEA PRESENT THEMSELVES TO THE WORLD WITH BRIGHTLY AND FULLY PAINTED FACES THAT BEFIT THE ABUNDANCE OF COLORS USED IN THEIR JEWELRY AND HEADDRESSES.

YOUNG MARUBO WOMAN

AMONG THE MARUBO OF WESTERN BRAZIL, BOTH WOMEN AND MEN PIERCE THE NASAL SEPTUM AND THREAD BEADED STRINGS THROUGH THE HOLE, THE BEADS BEING REGARDED AS A MEANS OF ATTUNEMENT TO THE NATURAL ENVIRONMENT OF WHICH THESE PEOPLE REGARD THEMSELVES AS CARETAKERS—NOT OWNERS.

PROTECTIVE MAKEUP

○

THE USE OF BLACK KOHL ON THE LOWER RIM OF THE EYE OF THIS NEPALI CHILD IS MEANT TO HELP PROTECT THE EYE FROM STRONG SUNLIGHT. THUS, ON A MEDICINAL LEVEL, THE MATERIAL ACTS AS A PROTECTION AGAINST VARIOUS DISEASES OF THE EYE AND, IN EXTENSION, IS THOUGHT TO BE A MAGICAL PROTECTION AGAINST THE EVIL EYE.

HENNA PASTE

○

CONVENIENTLY PACKAGED IN SMALL TUBES, HENNA PASTE CAN EASILY BE USED TO PAINT THE HANDS, ARMS, AND FEET. LESS PERMANENT THAN A TATTOO, THE DESIGNS LAST FOR ABOUT TWO WEEKS AND ARE ALSO USEFUL FOR TESTING THE APPEARANCE OF A REAL TATTOO. (PHOTOGRAPHED DURING THE AMSTERDAM TATTOO CONVENTION, 1996.)

SKIN ADORNMENT

○

AS IS CUSTOMARY FOR WOMEN AMONG MANY ISLAMIC PEOPLES FROM AFRICA TO INDIA, THIS YEMENITE WOMAN HAS ADORNED HER HANDS AND ARMS WITH HENNA PASTE. SUCH ADORNMENT IS REQUIRED NOT ONLY FOR A BRIDE AT HER MARRIAGE CEREMONY BUT ALSO IN PREPARATION FOR VARIOUS RELIGIOUS FESTIVALS.

social self and helps one's true self to emerge. Thus, masking, and temporarily obliterating, one's person (from the Greek *persona* for "mask") is, in fact, tribal therapy in action, and it therefore comes as no surprise that people masked or heavily made up often feel more free to dance in wild abandon, to be nude in public, and possibly even to make love to a complete stranger—all things that have occurred at large festivals during the last thirty years.

Somewhere between makeup and body painting are specialties and preferences that to some readers may seem unthinkable but that to others simply belong to their erotic imagination and/or practice. It was once fashionable, for example, for women to paint their nipples. The late eighteenth-century fashion for diaphanous blouses and very low-cut dresses lent itself perfectly to this practice, as would some of the more open and transparent women's garments of today.

Somewhere between body painting—an adornment that will be lost with the first rain, a dip into the river, or an extended shower—and the permanent tattoo we will discuss in the next chapter, there is an interesting custom of body decoration that results in tattoo-like designs lasting about two weeks. Using a paste made from henna, better known as a coloring agent for the hair, women in many countries across northern Africa, in Turkey, and in India use henna paste to adorn their hands and feet. Often a woman does this purely as a form of adornment and to enhance her beauty in order to attract the eyes of men. In some cases, however, the designs thus created are intended as magical protection against evil and disease—a significance that is usually found in the more permanent practice of the tattoo. After the henna paste is applied as shown on page 46, it dries, leaving a design in reddish orange or sometimes black, which remains visible for ten to fifteen days. Not only do the geometrical designs create the desired protection, but so does the henna itself. Apart from henna's medicinal quality as a cooling agent, henna is regarded as imbued with magical properties, foremost a sensitization that makes the wearer more receptive to the invisible yet omnipresent fields of energy in which we live. In this respect, the use of henna is very much related to the value placed on red ochre as blood of the earth by Australian Aborigines, Africans, and other ancient tribal cultures. This knowledge goes back to Neanderthal man at the dawn of history.

All in all, the great variety of body painting practices makes it clear that both the extended individual freedom of the late twentieth century and the relative anonymity of life in the great urban sprawl have contributed to the reemergence of an art form that is so essentially human as to have survived—with ups and downs—from the Stone Age to the present. It is quite possible that the future, if we believe the visions of science fiction writer William Gibson, of *Neuromancer* fame, will bring even more far-reaching ways of modification, in which computer chips will play a larger role than do the gold and precious stones that decorate the Kayan woman on page 54.

Although many body adornment practitioners today often seem to think that the choice of technique matters greatly—for example, scarification above tattooing or tattooing above painting—this is not true in all cases. Although the aspects of endorphin emission and attunement through pain involved in several techniques play their own role, the symbols and patterns inscribed or painted on the skin are certainly of equal importance. For example, Australian Aborigines—a people very much aware of the processes set in motion through cutting, blood, and pain—certainly do not use these techniques indiscriminately. As Robert Lawlor has shown in his detailed study, even temporary patterns "merely" painted rather than tattooed on the body have a clearly defined effect. Both at the time of initiation and immediately following death, Aborigines paint the person's clan totem design on the area between the nipples and the pubic region. The intricate pattern, so Lawlor says, "carries a vibrational affinity to a particular region in the sky where the ancestral source of that totem is said to reside. This resonance assists the soul of the deceased in reaching its ancestral dimension after death."[14]

Different in technique, yet similar in being an aid to establishing resonance, is the Australian practice of establishing psychic—that is, telepathic—contact with relatives by touching specific wounds created by earlier scarification; using the body's memory of the earlier pain to tap into deeper or higher levels of consciousness not normally accessible. Perhaps a similar rationale has given birth to the practice of blood brotherhood as practiced among Native Americans. Attuned by the mutual exchange of blood—actual body cells and molecules—the persons so bonded were then able to tap into a form of transmission between each other that is usually reserved for twins or for persons within the mother-child continuum.

DRESSING UP

AS DO MANY OF THE AMAZON
TRIBES, THE XINGU INDIANS PAINT
THEIR BODIES IN PREPARATION
FOR FESTIVE AND CEREMONIAL
OCCASIONS.

CEREMONIAL ADORNMENT

TWO YOUNG KAIAPO WOMEN FROM
MEKRANOTI FULLY ADORNED FOR
THEIR NAMING CEREMONY, AN
ANNUAL OCCASION DURING WHICH
CHILDREN'S NAMES ARE RITUALLY
CONFIRMED BY THE GROUP.

FEMALE FALCON
WIND ANGEL
✳ ⊙ ✳
IN THIS IMAGE, ARTIST NATASHA VON
ROSENSCHILDE BRINGS ALIVE A VISION
THAT MIGHT BE ENCOUNTERED DURING
THE SPIRIT-JOURNEY OF A NATIVE
AMERICAN BRAVE DURING AN
INITIATION, OR SIMPLY
IN A DREAM.

WARLPIRI WOMEN
✳ ⊙ ✳
AMONG THE AUSTRALIAN ABORIGINES,
BODY PAINTING IS NOT MERELY USED AS
AN ADORNMENT, BUT HAS RITUAL SIG-
NIFICANCE. THE WOMEN SHOWN HERE,
FROM THE WARLPIRI CLAN IN CENTRAL
AUSTRALIA, ARE ADORNED FOR A
DREAMTIME RITUAL.

ARTIST AND LIVING ART

AMONG THE ETHIOPIAN
SURI, MEN PAINT EACH
OTHER, INCLUDING
THE GENITALS, IN
PREPARATION FOR THEIR
REGULAR STICK FIGHTS.
THE RESULT OF THE
CAREFULLY EXECUTED
GENITAL ADORNMENT AT
RIGHT CAN BE SEEN
BELOW.

FIERCE WARRIOR
ᴏᴏᴏᴏᴏᴏ

AMONG THE TRIBES OF PAPUA NEW GUINEA, UNLIKE MOST CONTEMPORARY SOCIETIES IN THE EAST AND WEST, EXTENSIVE AND RADICAL MAKEUP IS NOT JUST THE PRESERVE OF WOMEN. IN HIS CULTURE, THIS WARRIOR'S IMAGE AS A "MAN" REMAINS FULLY INTACT, WHEREAS HERE PEOPLE WOULD LOOK AT HIM AND WONDER.

BERBER WOMAN
ᴏᴏᴏᴏᴏᴏ

THIS WOMAN OF THE AIT HADDIDU TRIBE, MOROCCO, COMBINES MAKEUP AND PERMANENT TATTOOS ON HER CHIN AND NOSE.

MAKEUP

MOST CONTEMPORARY MEN AND WOMEN WOULD DEFINE THESE TWO WHITE DOTS NOT AS MAKEUP BUT RATHER AS PART OF A BEAUTY MASK. TO THIS NAVAJO WOMAN FROM ARIZONA, HOWEVER, IT IS SIMPLY HER MAKEUP: A FACIAL DESIGN THAT MAKES HER FEEL AS BEAUTIFUL AND CONFIDENT AS EYELINER, LIPSTICK, AND ROUGE DO TO MANY WOMEN TODAY.

X-RAY VISION

COMPARABLE TO THE AFRICAN GIRL PICTURED ON PAGE 12, THE DESIGN WE SEE ON THIS WARRIOR FROM PAPUA NEW GUINEA IS NOT SIMPLY A SKELETON, BUT ATTESTS TO THE ABILITY OF MANY TRIBAL PEOPLE TO SEE BEYOND, OR INTO, NORMAL PHYSICAL APPEARANCES.

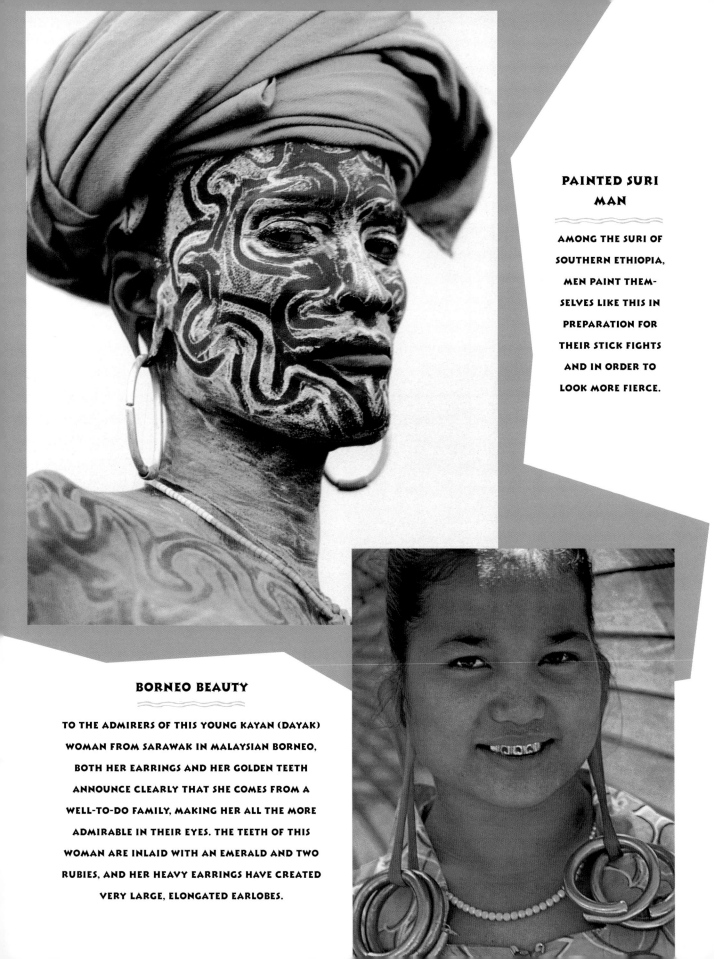

PAINTED SURI MAN

AMONG THE SURI OF SOUTHERN ETHIOPIA, MEN PAINT THEM-SELVES LIKE THIS IN PREPARATION FOR THEIR STICK FIGHTS AND IN ORDER TO LOOK MORE FIERCE.

BORNEO BEAUTY

TO THE ADMIRERS OF THIS YOUNG KAYAN (DAYAK) WOMAN FROM SARAWAK IN MALAYSIAN BORNEO, BOTH HER EARRINGS AND HER GOLDEN TEETH ANNOUNCE CLEARLY THAT SHE COMES FROM A WELL-TO-DO FAMILY, MAKING HER ALL THE MORE ADMIRABLE IN THEIR EYES. THE TEETH OF THIS WOMAN ARE INLAID WITH AN EMERALD AND TWO RUBIES, AND HER HEAVY EARRINGS HAVE CREATED VERY LARGE, ELONGATED EARLOBES.

As the above examples clearly show, and as we'll encounter equally often in the following chapters, many types of body adornment and body modification thus have little or nothing to do either with attaining an individual "look" or with conforming to a personal or social vision of "beauty." Rather, many of these techniques are aimed at awakening potentials of consciousness that are fully human and natural, rather than extrasensory or paranormal, but that need to be trained and activated just as our brains and muscles need to be trained and activated in order to function at their very best.

The Skin as Canvas

OF SPIRIT DRAWINGS AND GRAFFITI OF THE SOUL

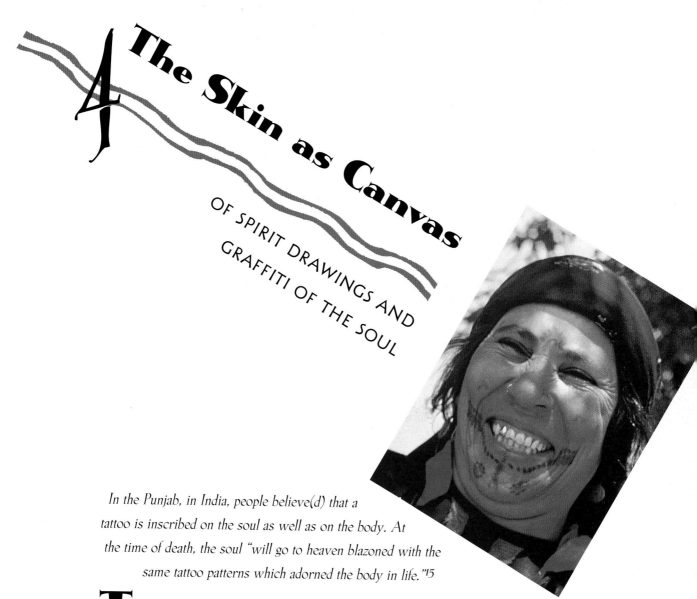

In the Punjab, in India, people believe(d) that a tattoo is inscribed on the soul as well as on the body. At the time of death, the soul "will go to heaven blazoned with the same tattoo patterns which adorned the body in life."15

THE ARTS OF TATTOOING and scarification have an extensive history and are distinguished by great cultural and artistic variety. The tattoo has been put to a truly wide spectrum of uses. Perhaps even more varied is the range of individual and collective motivations that have shaped this ancient art that is, and always has been, known in almost every region of the globe.

The most ancient tools for tattooing gave rise to the name *tattoo;* based on *tau tau:* the sound of the upper stick striking on the lower one during the application of a tattoo. The modern electric tattooing machine was not invented until 1891.

JAPANESE
FULL-BODY TATTOOS
❀ ❀ ❀
PAGE 56

ALTHOUGH IN JAPAN IT IS
MAINLY MEN WHO UNDER-
GO THE LENGTHY PROCE-
DURE OF HAVING THEIR
SKIN TURNED INTO SPLEN-
DIDLY PAINTED LIVING
CANVASES, HERE ARE TWO
WOMEN WHO HAVE MADE
THIS CHOICE. SUCH FULL-
BODY TATTOOS, OR
IREZUMI, CAN TAKE TWELVE
TO EIGHTEEN MONTHS OF
REPEATED VISITS TO THE
ARTIST, WHO IN THIS CASE
WAS THE ACCLAIMED
HORITOSHI I.

BEAUTY VERSUS EVIL
❀ ❀ ❀
PAGE 57

AMONG THE BEDOUIN
WOMEN OF JORDAN AND
ELSEWHERE, IT IS COMMON
KNOWLEDGE THAT FACIAL
TATTOOS NOT ONLY MAKE
THEM MORE BEAUTIFUL
AND ATTRACTIVE BUT ALSO
PROTECT THEM FROM EVIL
SPIRITS.

The various cultural and spiritual motivations for adorning the body with tattoos are legion. They range from the uniquely personal facial tattoos of the Maori to Cambodian or Thai spirit drawings meant to protect the wearer from harm; from a prisoner's simple graffiti to the works of art applied to the human body in both old and new Japan.

Before going into cultural detail about which people use tattoos, what designs they use, and their reasons for tattooing, I'd like to quote Henk Schiffmacher (Hanky Panky),* a practitioner, historian, and collector of the art who describes in only a few sentences the spectrum of circumstances that may lead to people becoming tattooed, whether in the context of tribal ritual or in a more casual or whimsical setting.

Tattoos can mark the occasion of either a victory or a defeat, can be an expression of joy or sorrow, performed as part of a ceremony or ritual and accompanied by mantras, song and dance. The phase of the moon may determine the time for a tattoo, as may also a particular constellation of the stars, or a season. Some people get themselves tattooed because of certain visions, taboos, oaths or injunctions. The decision to get a tattoo can be a voluntary, sober and well considered one, but there are also cases of tattoos being forced upon someone or performed in a moment of lighthearted spontaneity. The person may be confused, not responsible for their actions, drunk, mentally disturbed or under the influence of drugs. Sometimes, tattooing can have a religious background and at others times be the result of lust, sadism, torture or superstition.[16]

---

*"Hanky Panky," as Henk Schiffmacher is widely known, founded the Amsterdam Tattoo Museum in 1996.

TATTOOING TRADITIONAL STYLE

>>>>>>>>>>>>>>

THE RHYTHMIC SOUNDS EMERGING FROM USING THE MOST ANCIENT TOOLS FOR TATTOOING HAVE GIVEN RISE TO THE NAME *TATTOO*, BASED ON *TAU TAU:* THE SOUND OF THE UPPER STICK STRIKING ON THE LOWER ONE. ALTHOUGH TATTOOING TOOLS SHOW SLIGHT VARIATIONS ACROSS THE CULTURES OF SOUTHEAST ASIA AND OCEANIA, THE BASIC DESIGN AND TECHNIQUE ARE VERY MUCH THE SAME. (PHOTOGRAPHED CIRCA 1930, BORNEO.)

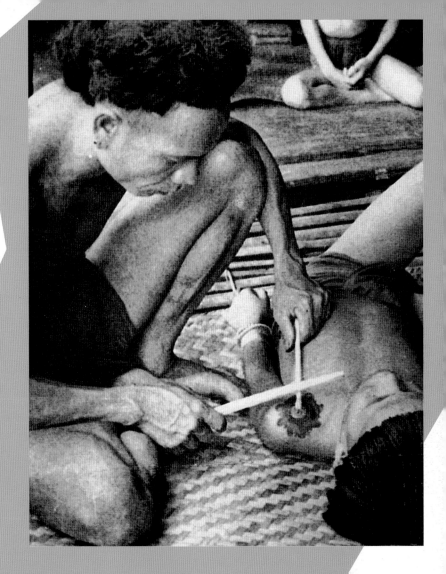

JAPANESE MASTER AT WORK

>>>>>>>>>>>>>>

FOR CENTURIES, JAPANESE TATTOO ADEPTS HAVE USED TRADITIONAL TOOLS WHEN APPLYING THEIR BEAUTIFUL ARTWORK TO THE SKINS OF THEIR CLIENTS. TODAY, HOWEVER, THE SPEED OF MODERN ELECTRICAL DEVICES AS WELL AS THEIR BEING LESS PAINFUL HAS CONVINCED EVEN THE TRADITION-MINDED JAPANESE. DURING THE AMSTERDAM TATTOO CONVENTION IN 1996, TATTOO-MASTER HORIWAKA, FROM TOKYO, GAVE A DEMONSTRATION OF HIS SKILLS USING CONTEMPORARY TOOLS AND INK.

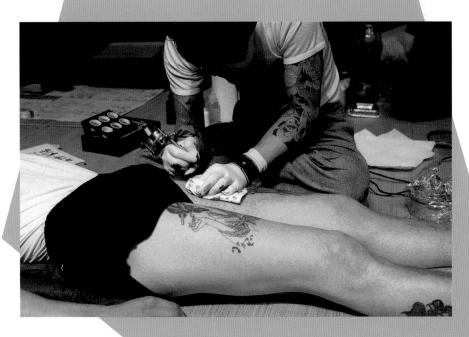

Although one can say, in general, that no part of the human body has not been used as a living piece of canvas for a tattoo or some other marking, the available literature and photographs make it clear that the face is least frequently marked, and then usually with small designs only. The reason for this is twofold. First, incising or puncturing the face or neck is one of the more painful experiences one can have with a tattoo, and pain—for most people—is not the major reason for getting a tattoo in the first place. Second, an undoubtedly stronger argument against facial tattooing is of a psychological and social kind. Whereas other tattoos can usually be hidden under clothing, the major rationale for the general form of the Japanese *irezumi* (see page 56), the face is always visible to the outside world. Given the history of the tattoo, which has so often been outlawed and declared illegal, a facial tattoo could easily get one into trouble. The most notable exception to this general rule is found in the facial designs of Maori men, and to a lesser degree in the lip and chin tattoos worn by women among both the Maori (page 62), and the Ainu of northern Japan (page 63).

Contemporary neotribals should, however, be aware that it just won't do to copy a Maori tattoo, however beautiful, from a book and have it inscribed onto the face. To a Maori man, his tattoo both is personal and enhances the natural features of his face and character. In the case of women with chin tattoos, these are often based in family tradition and are, in a very real sense, protected by copyright. Shannon Larratt of BME *(Body Modification Enzine)* puts it this way: "A Western comparison would be if you stole the seal of a royal family and made it your own family seal," and Tom Brazda of Stainless Studios adds, "When Westerners adopt a variation of the moko, the female moko which is just on the chin, the Maori say it insults their women and upsets their ancestors. If a European is seen wearing a female moko, he risks getting beat up."[17]

Although the tattoo is presently undergoing not only a renaissance but a period of full bloom in most cities and countries of the urbanized world, other societies are just now banning the practice. In Thailand, for example, where it once was most normal to be tattooed, government jobs are closed to anyone wearing a tattoo. This is comparable to efforts by other countries that on their emergence from the third world into the modern mainstream try to repress and forget aspects of their cultural heritage that were once thought of as primitive by the missionaries and

KALINGA TATTOOS

YOUNG FILIPINA WOMAN WITH THE HONEYCOMB PATTERN TATTOO OFTEN SEEN IN THE PHILIPPINE ISLANDS.

THE ILLUSTRATED WOMAN

DETAILED FULL-BODY TATTOOS ARE FOUND NOT ONLY IN JAPAN. ALTHOUGH IN THE WEST THEY ARE MORE RARE, THE AMOUNT OF WORK, PATIENCE, PAIN, AND COST INVOLVED ARE VERY MUCH THE SAME. ONLY THE STYLES DIFFER GREATLY.

NUDE OR NOT?

A TYPICAL EXAMPLE OF THE STYLE OF TATTOOING FOUND IN THE MARQUESA ISLANDS AND IN SAMOA. FOLLOWING WELL-DEFINED RULES ABOUT WHICH DESIGNS ARE EXECUTED AT WHAT AGE, A SAMOAN MAN, AS SHOWN HERE, WILL HAVE THE COMPLETE, INTRICATE PATTERN ONLY WHEN OLD.

MAORI WOMAN
✂◯✂
THIS TRADITIONAL CHIN
TATTOO DATES FROM
ABOUT 1900.

MAORI MOKO
✂◯✂
MAORI MAN WITH
TRADITIONAL MOKO
(FACIAL TATTOO),
DATING FROM
ABOUT 1900.

NO NEED FOR LIPSTICK

AINU WOMEN ENLARGE AND ENHANCE THEIR LIPS PERMANENTLY
BY MEANS OF A TATTOO, AS SHOWN IN THIS PHOTOGRAPH (LEFT)
FROM 1903, RATHER THAN BY MAKEUP APPLIED DAILY.

MIGHT THERE BE AN ANCIENT CONNECTION BETWEEN THE AINU
PEOPLE OF THE JAPANESE ISLAND OF HOKKAIDO AND THE MAORI
OF PRESENT-DAY NEW ZEALAND? AMONG BOTH PEOPLES, WOMEN
TATTOO AND THUS VISUALLY ENLARGE THEIR LIPS.

TE AHO TE RANGI WHAREPU

THIS CHIEF OF THE NGATI-MAHUTA TRIBE HAS A TYPICAL MAORI
MOKO, OR PERSONAL FACIAL TATTOO. SOMETIMES SUCH A MOKO
MAY APPEAR TO SOMEONE IN A DREAM, BUT THE ACTUAL TATTOO
IS CREATED ONLY WHEN THE COUNCIL OF ELDERS HAS DECIDED
THAT IT ACTUALLY DOES FIT THE PERSON.

traders of the West. As Thailand cracks down on tattoos, so does Malaysia on the beliefs and ritual practices of its folk religion and on the lengthened earlobes of its original inhabitants. Similarly, though on another continent, many African nations try to inhibit their people's ancient traditions of scarification and other types of body adornment and modification.

As with many other types of body adornment, present-day motivations for getting a tattoo differ somewhat from those of our ancestors and of most contemporary tribal people. Whereas the early Neolithic hunters of Europe and Central Asia most certainly applied spirit drawings to the skin with religious and magical intentions, and whereas the Egyptians of 2000 B.C.E. probably combined ritual demands for tattooing with a desire to enhance their attractiveness, today's neotribals show a wide spectrum of motivations.

Among contemporary tribal peoples, the Dayaks and other inhabitants of Southeast Asia provide a good example of how tattoos are not mere decorations but constitute an actual symbolic language instead (see pages 66–67). These peoples allowed only a proven warrior to wear a certain tattoo. Special designs on traditionally determined places of his body would show that he had killed beast or man, or that he was a man with an otherwise less visible adornment: the famous genital piercing known as ampallang (see *ampallang* in the Glossary).

However, in the absence of a clearly defined symbolic code in which tattoos are, in fact, a pictorial language, people now often wear tattoos that have been carefully and personally designed (see pages 68–71). Among them are many icons of current media fame such as Ninja Turtles, Mickey Mouse, pop stars, and even brand names, not to mention the many eagles, anchors, and nude women once characteristic of soldiers and sailors.

A striking example of a tattoo that seems truly a return to the tribal is shown on page 70. Author Deena Metzger has a unique tattoo that is representative of the symbolical and magical consciousness usually found among tribal people rather than twentieth-century contemporaries. Once the scar left by the mastectomy of her right breast had sufficiently healed on a physical level, this remarkable woman covered it with the design of a living and budding branch. In her book *Tree*, Metzger makes it quite clear that this symbol of life is meant to override the loss her body suffered at the hand of the surgeon. She describes the tattoo and its symbolism thus:

. . . where a knife entered, now a branch winds about the scar and travels from arm to heart. Green leaves cover the branch, grapes hang there and a bird appears. What grows in me now is vital and does not cause me harm. I think the bird is singing. I have designed my chest with the care given to an illuminated manuscript. I am no longer ashamed to make love. In the night, a hand caressed my chest and once again I came to life. Love is a battle I can win. I have the body of a warrior who does not kill or wound. On the book of my body, I have permanently inscribed a tree.[18]

Whereas this somewhat reminds us of the ways tribal people often fought psychological pain with physical pain (see chapter 6), others among today's neourban tribals simply base their designs on traditional ones. A particular form of neotribal style is based in the traditional designs of the Pacific and Southeast Asia yet has transformed them into truly modern and often very elegant patterns that seem both magical and intended to captivate the eye.

In considering again the various known motivations for tattooing the body, it becomes clear that the contemporary return to the tribal represents a swing of the pendulum of history, another loop in the continuous flow of time. Humanity, on reaching the end of one cycle and entering a new one, is more open to change at such crucial moments and seems to become sensitive yet again. Wrongly foreseen in the 1960s as a "New" or "Aquarian" age brought about by stellar constellations, what we currently witness is a reemergence of the tribal spirit from within the human psyche: genetic memory manifesting itself. Amid the concrete and silicon with which we've fashioned our world, the mythical serpent of the dreamtime is once again arising, reminding and recalling us to roots almost forgotten.

Whether some people now adorn their bodies in an attempt to belong to a certain group or "tribe," or others do so as an outward sign that they do not want to belong to a society in which all are all too equal, is not the major point. These are merely the confusions of a new childhood. What *is* important is that those who heed the call do not simply copy—or even steal—symbols, practices, and rituals from cultures of the past and tribal peoples of the present, but rather, as the New Zealand Maori, Native Americans, and other peoples have invited them to do, either come and ask and learn, or develop their own by simply turning within and listening patiently and quietly to the myriad voices of self and universe.

IBAN DAYAK

>>>>>>>>>>>

IN ADDITION TO THE TRADITIONAL
TATTOOS ON HIS THROAT AND SHOUL-
DERS MARKING HIM AS AN EXPERIENCED
WARRIOR, THIS DAYAK MAN FROM
MALAYSIAN BORNEO HAS AN UNUSUAL
MARKING ON HIS FOREHEAD, WHERE
EACH OF THE THREE DOTS REPRESENTS
ONE FOREIGN COUNTRY HE HAS
TRAVELED TO.

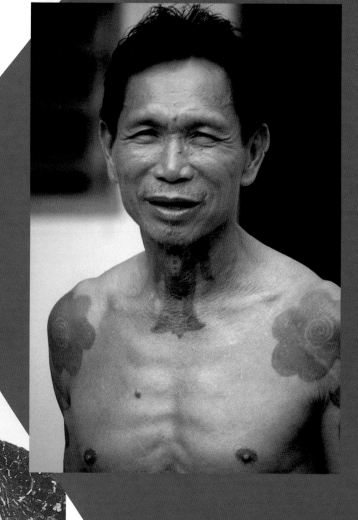

WOODABE WOMAN

ALTHOUGH TATTOOING IS MUCH LESS
COMMON THAN SCARIFICATION AMONG
DARK-SKINNED PEOPLE, THE WOMEN OF
SOME AFRICAN TRIBES USE TATTOO AS
BOTH AN ADORNMENT AND A MEANS OF
MAGICAL PROTECTION. THE TRIANGULAR
CHIN TATTOO OF THIS WOODABE WOMAN,
FOR EXAMPLE, IS MEANT TO GUARD HER
AGAINST THE EVIL EYE.

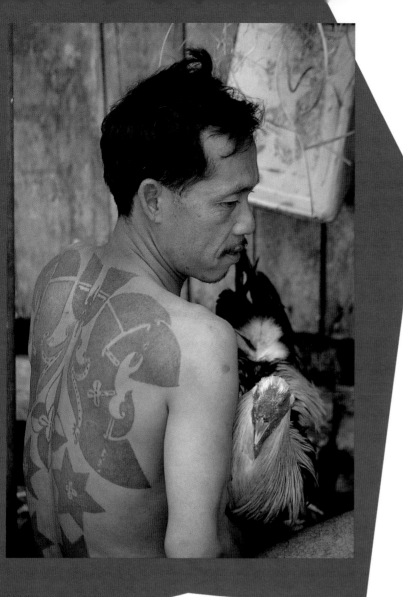

BORNEO TATTOO

MANY AMONG THE YOUNGER GENER-
ATION OF DAYAKS DO NOT FOLLOW
THE ANCIENT TRIBAL CODE OF TAT-
TOOING ANYMORE AND PREFER—IF
AT ALL—COMMON WESTERN DESIGNS
SUCH AS NUDE WOMEN OR CHINESE
DESIGNS SUCH AS DRAGONS. THIS
YOUNG DAYAK MAN, HOWEVER, HAS
DECIDED TO FOLLOW THE ANCIENT
WAYS ON HIS BACK, WHEREAS HIS
CHEST HAS A MODERN DESIGN.

PONYO NAGA

>>>>>>>>>>>

LIVING IN ASSAM AND BURMA, THE NAGAS
WERE INFAMOUS HEAD-HUNTERS. THE TWO
SYMBOLIC HUMAN FIGURES TATTOOED ON THIS
MAN'S CHEST REVEAL HIS HAVING KILLED TWO
MEN, WHICH GIVES HIM GREAT STATUS WITHIN
HIS GROUP. TODAY, NAGAS FREQUENTLY
ABSTAIN FROM TATTOOING BUT HAVE
PRESERVED THEIR TRADITIONAL DESIGNS AS
PATTERNS ON THEIR CLOTHING.

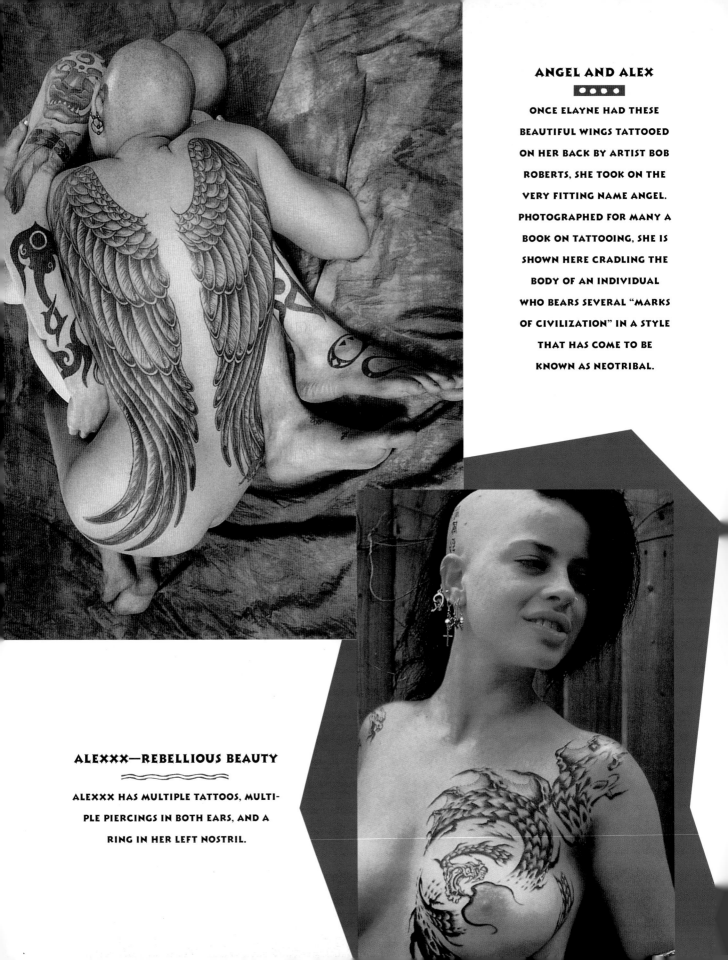

ANGEL AND ALEX

▪ ▪ ▪ ▪

ONCE ELAYNE HAD THESE BEAUTIFUL WINGS TATTOOED ON HER BACK BY ARTIST BOB ROBERTS, SHE TOOK ON THE VERY FITTING NAME ANGEL. PHOTOGRAPHED FOR MANY A BOOK ON TATTOOING, SHE IS SHOWN HERE CRADLING THE BODY OF AN INDIVIDUAL WHO BEARS SEVERAL "MARKS OF CIVILIZATION" IN A STYLE THAT HAS COME TO BE KNOWN AS NEOTRIBAL.

ALEXXX—REBELLIOUS BEAUTY

ALEXXX HAS MULTIPLE TATTOOS, MULTI-PLE PIERCINGS IN BOTH EARS, AND A RING IN HER LEFT NOSTRIL.

DOUBLE NIPPLE PIERCING

WHETHER OR NOT ONE WOULD WANT
A COCK TATTOOED ON THE CHEST,
ONE MUST RECOGNIZE THAT THE
WORK ITSELF, BY A. OVERSBY, HAS
BEEN BEAUTIFULLY EXECUTED. NOTE
ALSO HOW THE COCKEREL SEEMS TO
GRAB THE VERY SAME NIPPLE THAT
HAS BEEN PIERCED TWICE. THE
WEARER, SO IT WOULD SEEM, LOVES
TO FEEL THE BIRD'S TALONS.

ARTISTIC HAND

MIXING A TRIBAL DESIGN (ON THE
WRIST) WITH PLAYFUL FANTASY, THIS
ALMOST FEMALE-LOOKING HAND
IS, IN FACT, THE HAND OF A
BALINESE MAN.

BODY ART GOES MAINSTREAM

⬤⬤⬤⬤⬤⬤

RECENT YEARS HAVE BROUGHT AN EXPLO-
SION OF INTEREST IN—AND DEMAND FOR—
ALL TYPES OF BODY DECORATION, THOUGH
IT IS MAINLY TATTOOING, FOLLOWED BY
PIERCINGS OF ALL KINDS, THAT HAS
UNDERGONE A TRUE RENAISSANCE. ONCE
THE DOMAIN OF PEOPLE AT THE FRINGE OF
SOCIETY, TATTOOING IS BECOMING AS
ACCEPTABLE AS USING LIPSTICK OR
HAVING A FACE-LIFT.

SYMBOLIC HEALING

AUTHOR DEENA METZGER, HERE PHOTO-
GRAPHED BY HELLA HAMMID, HAS HAD
HER MASTECTOMY SCAR COVERED WITH
THE DESIGN OF A LIVING BRANCH.

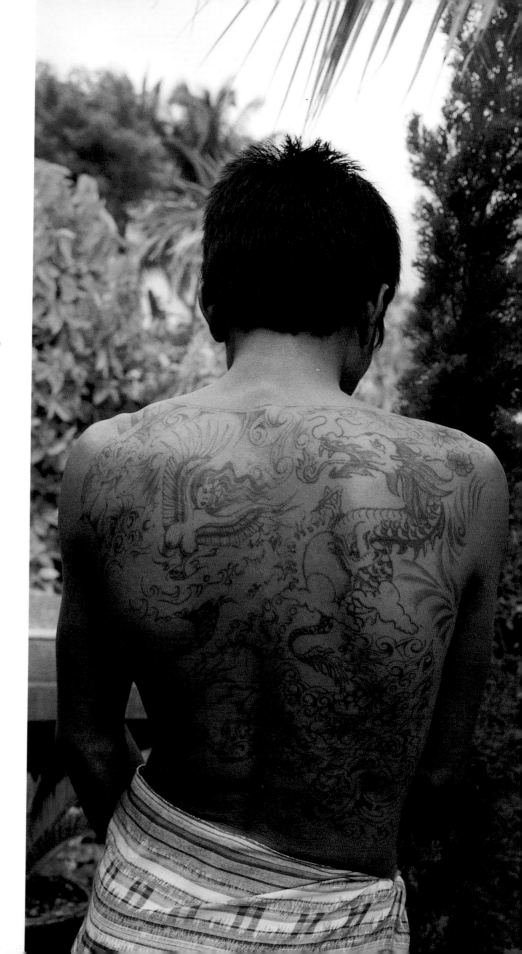

SISCA
✖ ⬤ ✖

BY HIS OWN ADMISSION,
THE YOUNG BALINESE
MAN IN THIS PHOTO-
GRAPH IS SUSPECT TO
VANITY AND LOVES TO
SHOW OFF HIS MULTIPLE
TATTOOS. WHEREAS HIS
MOST PAINFUL EXPERI-
ENCES TO DATE WERE THE
TATTOOS OF HIS EAR AND
EYEBROWS (SEE PAGE 1),
THE MOST EXPENSIVE AND
TIME-CONSUMING ONE
WAS ON HIS BACK. SISCA,
AN EX-TRANSVESTITE
NOW SELLING GARMENTS
ON BALI'S LOVINA BEACH,
IS ONE OF THOSE
NEOTRIBAL PEOPLE WHO
SPEND MOST OF THEIR
SPARE CHANGE ON
ACQUIRING MORE AND
MORE TATTOOS. AS WITH
MANY OTHER SUCH PEO-
PLE, HIS MOTIVATION IS
NOT MERE VANITY OR
EXHIBITIONISM BUT AN
ATTEMPT TO COMBAT OLD
PSYCHIC PAINS WITH NEW
PHYSICAL ONES AND TO
LEARN ONCE MORE TO
TRUST A STRANGER (THE
TATTOO ARTIST) AFTER
HAVING BEEN DISAP-
POINTED BY TOO MANY
OTHERS.

5 The Invisible Self

EROTIC ADORNMENT AND MODIFICATION

MOST READERS of this book live in contemporary Western or Westernized societies and have become entirely accustomed to the convention that life is lived within clothes. Hence, most of our bodies are concealed from others most of the time.

To many tribal peoples, however, and especially to the great number of those who live in tropical and subtropical regions, such a dichotomy between visible and invisible has never existed. Whereas the body adornments of the man and woman shown on page 72 are visible to everyone all the time, even though they are of an erotic nature, the equally elaborately adorned woman on page 75 would be seen as she is here only by her lover were it not for such publications as this and for other developments we shall discuss later on and in chapter 6.

So the moment any type of adornment, decoration, or enhancement goes beyond the face and limbs, it involves full or partial nudity, both when it is acquired and when it is shown to others or to the camera. Although nudity in itself is not necessarily erotic or sexual, except to true religious fundamentalists, most invisible adornments are motivated specifically by the erotic–sexual impulse. They include the piercing of nipples and navels, tattooing the pubic region, scarification done for tactile reasons, and branding as a sign of possession or submission in the BDSM (bondage/domination, submissive/master) setting.

Even more clearly sexual is the adornment or enhancement that involves piercing and/or restyling the genitals. Apart from the nipples, in fact, these most delicate parts of the invisible self seem to be the sites primarily chosen for such adornments and enhancements.

With few exceptions, this focus on the genitals is not gleaned from tribal peoples. Although there are hints in literature that Indian women used to pierce their inner or outer labia and that both Indian and Polynesian women tattooed their pubic areas, no photographic material seems to exist to document these facts.

What is clearly known is that the female labia minora—the small, inner genital labia—have been adorned and/or enlarged in some cultures. Among the Hottentot people, a woman was judged beautiful and powerful if she had large inner labia extending far beyond the outer ones. They were purposely elongated with weights and by daily manipulation and have been reported to be very large indeed. Early ethnologists called this modification the Hottentot apron. Other African tribes, such as the Basuto, Dahomey, Tonga, Urua, and Venda people, have followed the same practice, as have contemporary women in both the East and West. Considering that recently modern women have also begun to modify their labia (see *labia lift* and *labia removal* in the Glossary), we should recognize this as a clear return of the tribal, a shaking off of two thousand years of the Christian teaching that one may not tamper with either one's body or one's life.

FULLY ADORNED

AMONG CONTEMPORARY OR
MODERN PRIMITIVES, AND ALSO
AMONG PEOPLE NOT FITTING
THIS CATEGORY BUT WHO ARE
AESTHETICALLY ADVENTUROUS,
THE PRACTICES OF TATTOOING
AND PIERCING ARE OFTEN
COMBINED. THE RESULT IS NOT
ALWAYS AS TASTEFUL AS THAT
SHOWN HERE, WHERE A PIERCED
NAVEL, NIPPLES, AND GENITALS
ARE COMBINED WITH A TATTOO
TRULY BEFITTING THE BODY OF
ITS WEARER.

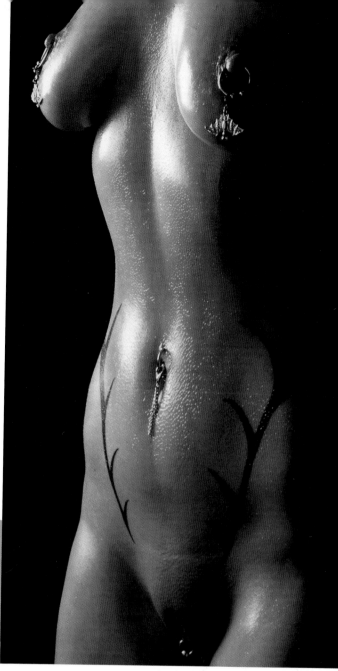

MURSI MAN

AMONG THE MURSI OF ETHIOPIA, SCARIFIED FACES AS
WELL AS BODIES ARE COMMON IN BOTH GENDERS.
THESE MEN AND WOMEN SEE THE PRACTICE AS AN
EROTIC ART RATHER THAN AS A MEANS OF SHOWING
TRIBAL IDENTITY OR PERSONAL HISTORY, AS AMONG
OTHER TRIBES. TO THE MURSI, THEIR SCARS ARE
MEANT TO ATTRACT THE OPPOSITE SEX AND ACT AS A
TACTILE ENHANCEMENT OF THE SKIN
DURING SEXUAL PLAY.

KARO
SCARIFICATIONS

AMONG THE KARO OF
ETHIOPIA, THE WELTS RAISED
BY BODY SCARIFICATION NOT
ONLY ARE REGARDED AS
VISUAL ENHANCEMENT OF
BEAUTY BUT ALSO ARE VAL-
UED FOR THEIR TACTILE
EROTIC QUALITY.

PUBIC TATTOO

PUBIC TATTOOS ARE RARELY SEEN, YET—ACCORD-
ING TO TATTOO ARTISTS—ARE DONE MORE OFTEN
THAN WE IMAGINE. THIS WOMAN HAS TWO DRAG-
ONS GUARDING HER MOST INTIMATE OPENING.
ALTHOUGH IT IS IMPOSSIBLE TO JUDGE
CORRECTLY, IT ALSO SEEMS THAT SHE WEARS A
RING THROUGH HER CLITORIS—A PIERCING
THAT IS LESS COMMON BUT IS SAID
TO BE VERY STIMULATING.

The Invisible Self

Concerning tribal men, the best known and most interesting example of genital modification comes from the Dayak of Borneo, in both the Indonesian and Malaysian parts of the island. Here, a man would not be able to find a woman for love or life if he were to omit the piercing known as ampallang, the local name for a small metal shaft that is inserted in a hole bored through the penile glans. Although in scientific literature this form of piercing is often wrongly discussed with male circumcision, it has nothing to do with it. The ampallang is clearly a genital adornment and, according to those who really know, a means of genital enhancement. The practice is known not only in Borneo but also in other areas of Oceania, and it results in a phallus not only adorned but apparently more stimulating to a man's sexual partners. The local women equate making love to a man without an ampallang with the taste of plain rice, whereas sexual union with a man wearing one is seen as much more exciting; in their words, like rice with salt.* A visit to the Sarawak Museum in Kuching, Borneo, proved very enlightening. It was shown here that the ampallang practice originated as a means, both magical and practical, of acquiring the stamina and strength—perhaps even the size—of a rhinoceros. The two-horned rhinoceros (*Dicerus sumatrensis*) of Sumatra and Borneo has, a clearly visible, a small diagonal bone in his member, more or less like that of the neotribal on page 80. During maturity, by way of calcification through urine, this natural ampallang even grows in size—something that also happens to men who never take the metal shaft out of the flesh. Ampallang wearers—and here the invisible is made visible after all—announce their status by having a special mark tattooed on the shoulder.

To those practices that are both a visual adornment and a sexual enhancement belong also the various piercings shown on pages 78 and 80. Women with such piercings of the labia, clitoral hood, or clitoris itself very often report that the sensitivity of these parts is very much enhanced. In addition to this and the visual effect in general, piercings in the nipples and genitals—of both women and men— give rise to a whole new set of possibilities for playing with one's own body or

---

*A contemporary amapallang user, the American Fakir Musafar (b. 1930) discusses his experience with this implement in the book *Modern Primitives* by Vale and Juno.

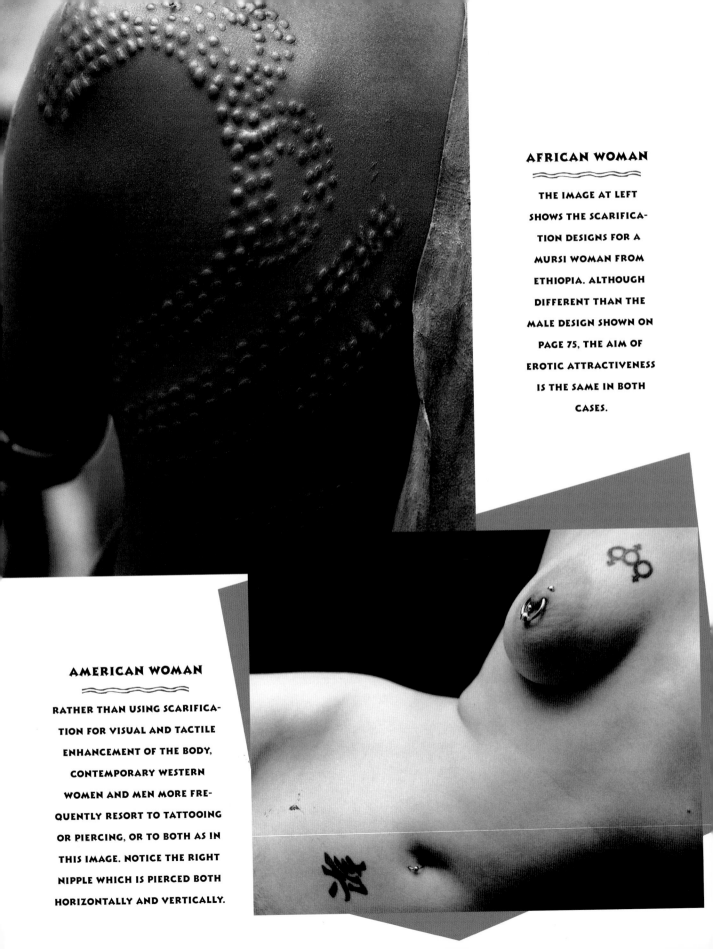

AFRICAN WOMAN

THE IMAGE AT LEFT
SHOWS THE SCARIFICA-
TION DESIGNS FOR A
MURSI WOMAN FROM
ETHIOPIA. ALTHOUGH
DIFFERENT THAN THE
MALE DESIGN SHOWN ON
PAGE 75, THE AIM OF
EROTIC ATTRACTIVENESS
IS THE SAME IN BOTH
CASES.

AMERICAN WOMAN

RATHER THAN USING SCARIFICA-
TION FOR VISUAL AND TACTILE
ENHANCEMENT OF THE BODY,
CONTEMPORARY WESTERN
WOMEN AND MEN MORE FRE-
QUENTLY RESORT TO TATTOOING
OR PIERCING, OR TO BOTH AS IN
THIS IMAGE. NOTICE THE RIGHT
NIPPLE WHICH IS PIERCED BOTH
HORIZONTALLY AND VERTICALLY.

that of a partner. The least common of all yoni piercings is that of the clitoris; yet, as an experienced piercer once said, "the women who have them love them." Piercings of both the clitoris and the skin of the hood are enhancements that not only amplify sensation but create new ones never before felt.

A practice that has—to my knowledge—not yet reappeared on the contemporary scene is the type of scarification done by several African tribes. Whereas most scarifications, as discussed previously, are merely visual, marking age and/or initiations undergone, some honest tribals and researchers have clearly stated that the actual scars are meant to attract the opposite sex. The Karo, especially (see page 76), regard the raised welts as a tactile enhancement of the skin during sexual play (see also pages 75 and 78).

So to many people what seem to be "mutilations" of the body, and especially of the genitals, are seen by the practitioners and often their consorts as adornments and even actual, practical enhancements. Lesser known than the examples given here—or at least not often spoken of—are many men's attempts at phallus elongation. Scrotal stretching, encasement, and constriction techniques are practiced by only a few men with a taste for radical adventure and experimentation.

In conclusion, let me focus on an often overlooked fact. Whereas some of the techniques and practices described here have been shown to have tribal antecedents, this is not the major issue. What is, to me, a clearer indication of the present return to tribal practices and consciousness lies in the fact that the invisible self is becoming more visible. Although many erotic, sexual, genital tattoos and piercings are done in privacy, behind the curtains of a piercing studio, many other neotribals choose to have them done in a semipublic situation. Often recreating a sense of ritual, such people lay bare to the group not only their skin but also their experience of both intense pain and intense pleasure. Whether or not the onlookers chant during the operation or welcome the newly adorned with applause and hugs afterwards, what we see in essence is a new member joining the tribe in a bond that is beyond family or nation or race or gender. Once more, and unlike the practices imposed by truly tribal people, it is the personal choice that differentiates the neotribal from all other peoples we usually designate by the term *tribal*.

During the growing number of conventions for the adorned, whether tattooed

PIERCED FRENUM

● ● ● ● ●

LESS FAMOUS THAN OTHER PENILE PIERC-
INGS, SUCH AS THE AMPALLANG OR THE
PRINCE ALBERT, A PIERCING OF THE
FRENUM IS EASY AND NOT VERY PAINFUL.
APART FROM SERVING THE AIM OF BEAUTI-
FICATION, MANY GENITAL PIERCINGS
PROVIDE ADDITIONAL TACTILE
STIMULATION FOR BOTH PARTNERS
DURING SEXUAL PLAY.

INTIMATE JEWELRY

● ● ● ● ●

IN THIS DRAWING, ARTIST CHRISTINA
CAMPHAUSEN SHOWS HOW THE DELICATE
INNER LABIA CAN LOOK ONCE THEY
ARE PIERCED AND ELONGATED BY
TINY WEIGHTS.

CAUCASIAN NEOTRIBAL MAN

● ● ● ● ●

REMINISCENT OF PAPUA WARRIORS WITH BONES INSERT-
ED THROUGH THE NASAL SEPTUM, THIS PRESENT-DAY
RADICAL HAS CHOSEN A LESS CONSPICUOUS PLACEMENT
FOR HIS PERSONAL TOTEM. ONE LESSON TO BE DRAWN
FROM THE MANY CONTEMPORARY PUBLICATIONS ON
THE TOPIC OF BODY DECORATION AND RADICAL
SEXUALITY IS THIS: THERE IS NO SINGLE SOCIAL
STRATUM TO WHICH THE PRACTITIONERS BELONG. THIS
MAN COULD BE YOUR NEIGHBOR, THE BANK MANAGER
DECIDING WHETHER OR NOT YOU GET YOUR CREDIT, OR
THE GROCER AT THE CORNER.

or pierced, as well as at thousands of discos and private parties, more and more people go beyond mainstream conventions of dress and behavior to show more of themselves—especially more of their usually hidden and invisible selves. In extension—and if done with maturity and self-knowledge—the person actually *becomes* herself or himself more truly than is usually possible and allowed by society in general. What we witness, in fact, is a new phase in coming out, but one unrelated to gender or issues of gender-oriented sexual preference.

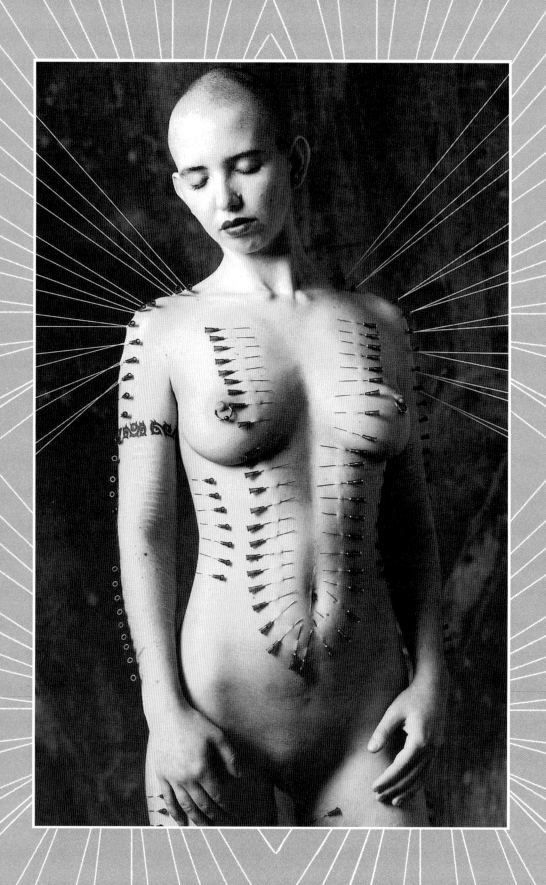

Losses and Gains

ATONEMENT BY SACRIFICE AND ATTUNEMENT BY PAIN

IN MOST PRESENT-DAY SOCIETIES, the concept of pain is purely negative: pain is associated with suffering the consequences of either disease or aggression. As has been done with the realities of birth, sex, and death—the other "wet" and "dirty" truths that belong to human life—pain has been banned from discussion and experimentation and from everyday discourse. It is seen almost exclusively as something unwanted, as something to get rid of by all means and as soon as possible. Similarly, the concept of sacrifice has become mainly a material and/or psychological one. One may perhaps sacrifice one's career for a loved one or for a political cause, or one may sacrifice at the altar of a deity by giving flowers or some money, but hardly anyone now thinks it sane to sacrifice one's life or a part of one's body.

Although most of us perceive this concept as normal or even natural, this is by no means universally true. Other societies and cultures—historical, contemporary tribal, or even as modern as Japanese—have had very different attitudes toward both suffering and pain.

Although the practice is losing ground, it can still happen in contemporary Japan that a man who has made a truly grievous mistake and caused deep suffering to another will atone by cutting off a part of his finger. Hailing from the Samurai period with its strong views concerning allegiance and duty, this practice has survived among members of the Yakuza. Although it is in fact a criminal organization, the Yakuza has influenced most aspects of Japanese society so strongly as hardly to be a subculture. Yakuza members (who, by the way, love and promote the full-body tattoo), are known to be otherwise very conservative members of society with mainstream opinions and lifestyle.

Although the act of presenting the sacrificed part of one's finger to the person one is indebted to seems to indicate an act of symbolic compensation, it does not really compare with the financial compensation someone else may receive for the loss of a loved one through the actions of a third party. In the case of physical sacrifice, one must not overlook the dimension of atonement it carries for the giver himself. If fully human, someone who has caused great calamity, or even loss of life, needs to battle the demons of guilt. Physical pain, as is borne out by countless volumes of psychoanalytical literature and many novels, can be a great ally in such a battle, which often takes years until the person in question achieves a sense of atonement. In such a process, then, outwardly perceived as a mere loss, we can also perceive a gain.

Similar, although with a different motivation, is the practice employed by Australian Aborigines to deal with their pain at losing a loved one. Even when there is no personal guilt, but rather to alleviate grief over the loss, Aborigines may inflict deep wounds on themselves. Such thigh slashing is not the only pain-related practice among these peoples. Here, among perhaps the most ancient culture

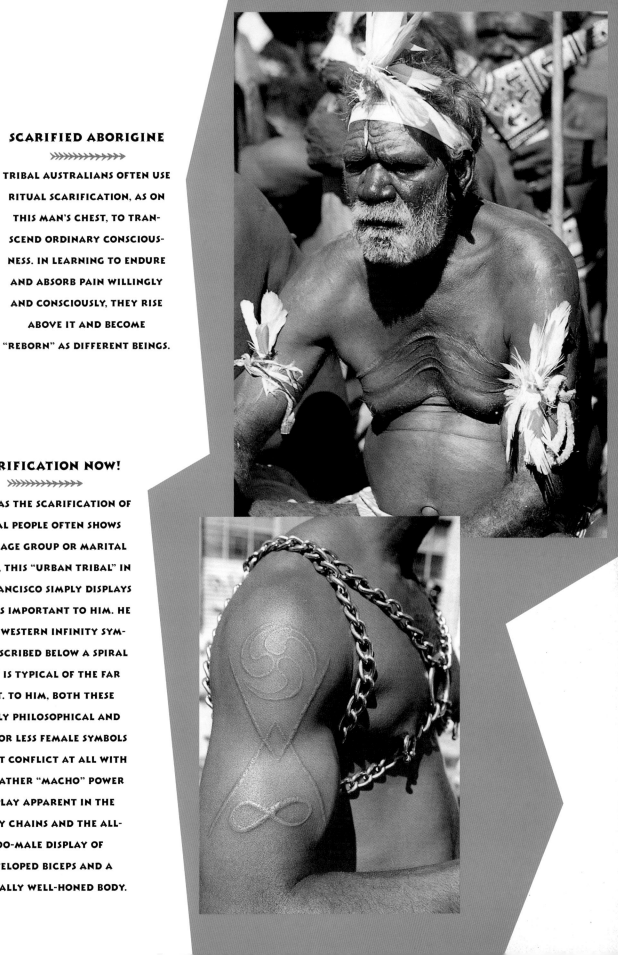

SCARIFIED ABORIGINE

⟫⟫⟫⟫⟫⟫⟫⟫⟫

TRIBAL AUSTRALIANS OFTEN USE
RITUAL SCARIFICATION, AS ON
THIS MAN'S CHEST, TO TRAN-
SCEND ORDINARY CONSCIOUS-
NESS. IN LEARNING TO ENDURE
AND ABSORB PAIN WILLINGLY
AND CONSCIOUSLY, THEY RISE
ABOVE IT AND BECOME
"REBORN" AS DIFFERENT BEINGS.

SCARIFICATION NOW!

⟫⟫⟫⟫⟫⟫⟫⟫⟫⟫⟫⟫

WHEREAS THE SCARIFICATION OF
TRIBAL PEOPLE OFTEN SHOWS
THEIR AGE GROUP OR MARITAL
STATUS, THIS "URBAN TRIBAL" IN
SAN FRANCISCO SIMPLY DISPLAYS
WHAT IS IMPORTANT TO HIM. HE
HAS A WESTERN INFINITY SYM-
BOL INSCRIBED BELOW A SPIRAL
THAT IS TYPICAL OF THE FAR
EAST. TO HIM, BOTH THESE
DEEPLY PHILOSOPHICAL AND
MORE OR LESS FEMALE SYMBOLS
DO NOT CONFLICT AT ALL WITH
THE RATHER "MACHO" POWER
DISPLAY APPARENT IN THE
HEAVY CHAINS AND THE ALL-
TOO-MALE DISPLAY OF
DEVELOPED BICEPS AND A
GENERALLY WELL-HONED BODY.

that has somewhat survived into the twentieth century, a person uses pain as a means of transcending ordinary consciousness, of opening the heart and mind to realities beyond everyday life. The extensive scars remaining from such rituals, as shown on page 85, will then forever mark that person as an experienced and adult member of the tribe—someone who can endure and possesses great self-discipline.

Strength, discipline, endurance, and bravery are often tested in those tribal societies, whose members often had to fight for survival either in a difficult climate or against neighboring peoples. Famous in this connection is the Sioux sun dance in which a young man had to prove his manhood by enduring the pain of hanging from eagle claws pierced through his chest muscles. Similar pains are suffered—not self-inflicted, but certainly voluntarily—by the men taking part in the yearly processions that occcur in India and Malaysia, in Penang—the Kavandi-bearers. Kavandi is an Indian term based on *kavaca* (a metal corselet and/or a coat of arms) and *kavadi* (a vow to make a pilgrimage). Kavandi-bearers undergo the most impossible looking tortures for this one day a year. They walk through the streets carrying heavy weights on their shoulders, their chests and backs often covered by flesh-hooks with weights attached. Others have knives or spears that puncture their cheeks or tongues. Yet, these people are not yogis, the "professionals" in renunciation of the body and transcendence of physical limits. On the day of the processions, one sees the shopkeeper from next door twisting through the street with his eyeballs rolling madly—asking the gods for better business—or the son of the old lady from across the street who hopes, by this suffering, to attract divine attention to his diseased mother by his physical prayer of pain. Trance-consciousness is so powerful that once the procession is over and the deities, in form of the priest, have accepted the offering, the wounds of the practitioners heal in a day and become simply invisible.

Less elaborate, more elegant, and perhaps with a different motivation (though unknown to me) is the exercise undergone by the women on page 82. Here too, she must be in a special state of mind in order to bear the pain of the insertion of multiple needles into her skin. Today, more and more urban and neotribal people have discovered new and old uses of pain, even beyond the S/M scene, both gay and straight, that have sprung up during the last years in most greater cities. In many of the recent publications concerning piercing and tattooing, modifying, or

**CAN YOU FEEL
IT?**

❀ O ❀

A RARE PHOTOGRAPH
SHOWING THE ACTUAL PROCESS
OF SCARIFICATION
AMONG THE NUBA, IN SUDAN.

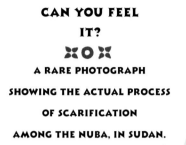

KAVANDI BEARER

❀ O ❀

DURING THE ANNUAL TAIPURAM
FESTIVAL, SOME OF THE YOUNG MEN
CARRY ELABORATE AND HEAVY CON-
TRAPTIONS DURING A PROCESSION TO
THE TEMPLE. THE MANY METAL SPIKES
ALL PIERCE THIS KAVANDI-BEARER'S
SKIN DURING THE LONG TRIP
THROUGH THE HEAT.

PIERCING AS MAGICAL PROTECTION

IN ADDITION TO THEIR LIP-PLUGS, KIRDI WOMEN OFTEN WEAR LONG INSERTS IN THEIR PIERCED EARS THAT ARE BELIEVED TO PROTECT THEM FROM "EVIL EXHALATIONS" OF SUPERNATURAL FORCES.

CLAY LIP-PLATE

AMONG THE SURI OF SOUTHWEST ETHIOPIA, IT IS THE WOMEN WHO WEAR LARGE LIP-PLATES. IN A PROCESS STARTING SIX MONTHS BEFORE MARRIAGE, A LIP-PIERCING IS CONTINUOUSLY ENLARGED, AND ITS FINAL SIZE AT MARRIAGE DETERMINES THE BRIDAL PRICE TO BE PAID BY THE FUTURE HUSBAND AND HIS FAMILY.

even customizing the human body, one finds statements concerning the conscious and mainly positive use of pain. In recent years, more and more people have attended the "ball dances" organized in various cities across the United States. Here, in the tradition of the Indian Taipusham festivals (see page 92) the more daring participants have balls hooked into their flesh and then dance until, as they say, the "flesh rips." Most who have undergone this new ritual of the "modern primitives movement" enthusiastically report on the liberating and transforming effects of the pain thus created and transcended.

Other gains, in the context of enduring pain and/or discomfort, come in many different and often surprising ways. Whereas the Padang girl on page 90 gains, with a certain loss of comfort and mobility, a safer economic future through tourists and their donations, the painful piercing of the upper ear on page 88 gains the bearer magical protection against evil. Where the women on pages 8, 83, and 88 lose their ability to speak and eat while wearing these huge lip-plates whenever they are in public situations, they gain in social status and command a higher bridal price at marriage. Similarly, the unfortunate girls on page 90 who are prepared for the loss of part of their genitals—I say unfortunate because I'm fully opposed to this practice—do, in fact, only then gain full membership in their particular society, and full status as marriageable woman.

Most surprising, however, are the indications that a certain piercing—namely that of the nasal septum—may have a very different rationale than a desire to look fierce or show off one's ability and willingness to endure the pain it entails. Widely practiced in Australia and Papua New Guinea, the nasal septum piercings seem to enhance or lead to the ability to have cross-sensual perception. What happens with this type of perception, often regarded as magical and/or paranormal, is that one or more of the five major senses expands into the realm of others. The widely traveled author Lyall Watson has described this phenomenon very adequately after a trip to some of the more remote Indonesian islands.[19] Here he encountered people who were able to see spoken words in the form of colored bubbles in the air. With nasal septum piercings, it seems that the sense of vision gets crossed with the sense of smell, once more leading to an ability that is usually either disbelieved fully or regarded as supernatural.

CLITORIDECTOMY

THESE TWO YOUNG GIRLS FROM THE IVORY COAST ARE BEING PAINTED IN PREPARATION FOR THE NOW CONTROVERSIAL CEREMONY OF CLITORIDECTOMY. NOT BEING INFORMED OF THE CONSEQUENCES, THEY ARE LED TO BELIEVE THAT THIS "INITIATION" TRANSFORMS THEM FROM GIRLS INTO WOMEN.

FROM GIRLHOOD TO WOMANHOOD

AT THE AGE OF TWELVE OR FOURTEEN, A PADANG GIRL'S NECK-RINGS ARE EXCHANGED FOR BIGGER AND HEAVIER COILS, WHICH MAKE HER A WOMAN. FROM THAT MOMENT ON, THE RINGS WILL NEVER BE TAKEN OFF AGAIN.

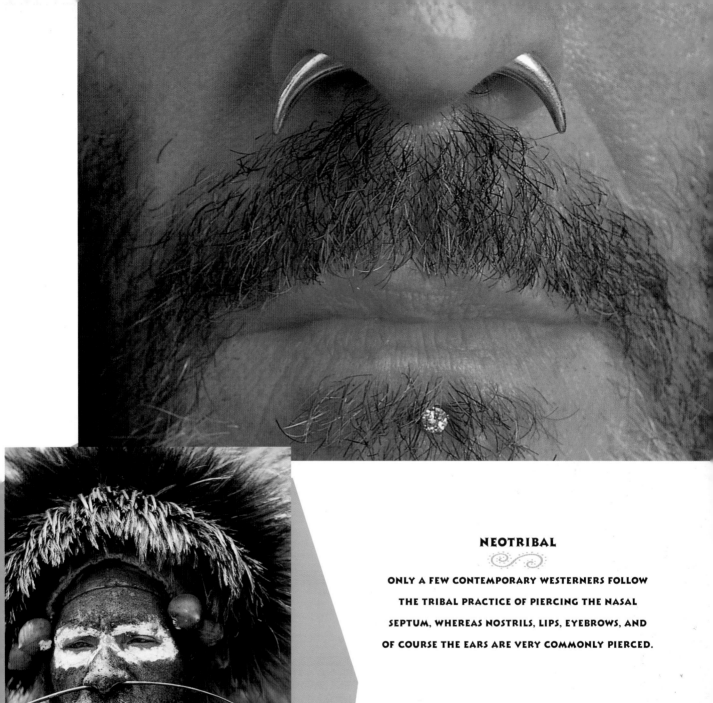

NEOTRIBAL

ONLY A FEW CONTEMPORARY WESTERNERS FOLLOW
THE TRIBAL PRACTICE OF PIERCING THE NASAL
SEPTUM, WHEREAS NOSTRILS, LIPS, EYEBROWS, AND
OF COURSE THE EARS ARE VERY COMMONLY PIERCED.

NEW GUINEAN WARRIOR

THE NASAL SEPTUM PIERCING, A FAVORITE AMONG
THE TRIBAL PAPUA OF NEW GUINEA, IS WIDESPREAD
AMONG THE MEN. JUST AS DIFFERENT INDIVIDUALS
USE DIFFERENT STYLES OF BODY PAINTING, SO DO THE
NASAL INSERTS VARY WIDELY, RANGING FROM BOAR
TUSKS TO TWIGS, FERN LEAVES, AND RINGS MADE
FROM MOTHER OF PEARL.

SELF-INITIATION—THE RADICAL PRIMITIVE

FAKIR MUSAFAR REENACTS HIS PERSONAL VERSION OF AN ANCIENT NATIVE AMERICAN RITUAL, THE "SUN DANCE." ALTHOUGH MANY NATIVE AMERICANS REGARD THIS AS A COMMERCIAL PROFANATION OF A SACRED PRACTICE, FAKIR'S VARIOUS PERFORMANCES, LECTURES, AND WRITINGS HAVE DONE MUCH TO AWAKEN PEOPLE'S INTEREST IN TRIBAL PRACTICES AND TO MAKE THEM AWARE OF THE TRANSFORMATIVE VALUE OF FEELING AND ENDURING PHYSICAL DISCOMFORT AND PAIN.

TAIPURAM FESTIVAL PROCESSION

ANNUALLY ONE CAN ENCOUNTER THIS FESTIVAL IN SEVERAL CITIES OF INDIA AND SOUTHEAST ASIA. HERE YOUNG HINDU MEN FROM PENANG, MALAYSIA, HAVE WEIGHTS HOOKED INTO THE SKIN OF THEIR CHEST AND ARE LED BY REIGNS ATTACHED TO THEIR BACK WITH FLESH-HOOKS IN ORDER TO ATTRACT DIVINE ATTENTION.

Perhaps future research will be able to locate the limits of both human perception and human endurance—*if* there are any limits at all. The current interest in, and return to, many tribal practices can only aid that process of learning to understand the human primate more fully than has been thought possible.

7

Our Genetic Memory

SEX AND DRUGS AND RITUAL

NOT ONLY IN THE REALM of body adornment do we find indications that what we are witnessing today is a return to the tribal. This does not mean an actual return to a fully tribal lifestyle or to a complete set of tribal values, but certainly to many tribal activities and sometimes to tribal ways of looking at the world.

Some visionaries have seen this coming, though they could not envision just how, in detail, this tribalization would come about and how it would express itself. Thirty years ago, in 1967, media sociologist Marshall McLuhan predicted that the new media (which then still meant radio and TV) and the new music (then rock 'n' roll and its psychedelic offsprings) would reawaken tribelike rituality, acted out in discos and festivals—the temples of the 1960s. No one, however, could have foreseen the force and inventiveness with which the ancient—against all odds—would find itself pathways into the present.

LOVE IS THE GAME

PAGE 94

AS MORE AND MORE INDI-
VIDUALS FULLY RECLAIM
CONTROL OVER THEIR BOD-
IES, A BASIC HUMAN RIGHT
OFTEN USURPED BY POLITI-
CAL OR RELIGIOUS GROUPS,
THEY REVIVE NOT ONLY
ANCIENT ARTS SUCH AS
TATTOOING AND PIERCING
BUT ALSO THE FREE EXPRES-
SION OF SEXUALITY IN ALL
ITS MANY FORMS. WHEREAS
"DEFIANT" WAS A LABEL OF
PRIDE IN THE 1960S, THE
1990S ALSO INTRODUCED
THE SPELLING "DEVIANT."
TOGETHER, IN THE DEFINI-
TION OF PAT CALIFIA, THESE
TWO SPELLINGS ADD UP TO
"SEX RADICAL."

**THERE PROCEEDS
SUPREME JOY**

PAGE 96

ANCIENT CULTURES IN
INDIA AND CHINA WERE
LESS ASHAMED OF THE BODY
AND SEXUALITY THAN WE
ARE TODAY. THE ART OF
THESE CULTURES DEPICTS
MANY FORMS OF EROTIC
PLAY, INCLUDING HOMOSEX-
UALITY AND MULTIPLE
PARTNERING.

Today, as the year 2000 approaches, sex, drugs, ritual, and rock 'n' roll play an even greater part in the social landscape than ever before in the industrialized world. Wherever we look for it, in almost every country—except those with no civil liberties at all—there are groups and workshops and gatherings in which, similarly to most tribal peoples, contemporary youths and adults experiment with altered states of consciousness. These practices are not very different from shamanism, which used to refer only to the religious, magical, and trance-inducing practices of Siberian tribal peoples. However, since comparative religion has established that equivalent techniques were known and used in tribal cultures across the globe, shamanism has become a generic term for all the techniques described here. Very much in its tradition, such expanded states are often induced by one or more of the well-known and ancient techniques to induce trance: music, dance, sensory deprivation or overload, drugs, sexuality, or most often a combination of two or more of these separate pathways that lead beyond the ego and beyond the socially programmed masks most of us wear.

An equally unforeseen reemergence of the tribal spirit, and of tribal values, can be detected when we look at the many expressions of what is often called the ecological movement. Whether individuals and groups spend much of their lives, love, and energy for whales or dolphins, or whether they return to ways of farming without the modern aids of poisonous fertilizers, knowingly or not they are guided by the tribal spirit.

I feel that we must preserve the ecology, but that we must go beyond the mere preservation of mineral, vegetable, and animal kingdoms—we must at any cost preserve the natural caretakers of these kingdoms and thus ourselves—we must preserve and relearn from the indigenous people and their ways. We must look to the primitive [primal/first], the so-called savages, pagans, or heathens of the world if we are going to survive the environmental catastrophe we have set in motion with our greed, technological and industrial interests fed by a total lack of appreciation and respect for the basic principles of life.

We are . . . the greatest embodiment of the One Spirit of Life. The growing Neo-Primitive consciousness in occidental society is evidence of a positive return to the primal and divine nature of that unique life in each human being. Further, this is expressive of our latent but inherent primitivity, i.e. the tribal animism and totemism inspired by our primitive foreparents for our survival.

Baaba, Neo-primitive researcher and educator[20]

The same principle applies to many things and groups that have reemerged during the last decades: religion and ritual centered on the goddess, the newly awakened concern for whole and healthy food, the rediscovery of herbal medicines that have been used by tribal peoples from Siberia to Australia and from Canaan to China.

In the wake of herbal rediscoveries, the last two generations of Western youths and adults have also rediscovered the great variety of consciousness-altering plant substances. Although there is most certainly a widespread ignorance of how to use these substances wisely, it has also become very clear—sometimes through the guidance of tribal initiates—that the informed and conscious use of such psychopharmacologic agents can be very beneficent, both to the individual and to the group partaking in the ceremonial use of these "drugs." Other than the major legal drugs today, such as alcohol, nicotine, coffee, and chocolate, "tribal" drugs made from mushrooms, herbs, and vines are not ingested for self-gratification. Rather, their value lies in their ability to sensitize the body and mind, heighten perception, and help the user gain insights into self and others. Used with intelligence and wisdom, they even open certain doors on the path to spiritual awakening. It is for this very reason that, try as one might, the use of these substances—as of all the tribal ways and techniques—has prevailed throughout history and will prevail into the future.

It is no coincidence that often one specific expression of this return to the tribal comes as part and parcel of a whole group of originally tribal techniques, though outwardly—at first glance—they may not seem related: ritually ordered celebrations, the use of trance-inducing music (especially drumming and chanting) whether or

PUBLIC NUDITY
›››››››››››››

A YOUNG WOMAN IS
CARRIED AWAY ON THE
WAVES OF MUSIC IN SAN
FRANCISCO'S
GOLDEN GATE PARK
(CIRCA 1970).

RITUAL NUDITY
›››››››››››››

HARKING BACK TO
ANCIENT PRACTICES,
THE EIGHT MEN AND
WOMEN IN THIS IMAGE
PERFORM A DANCE THAT
IS EQUALLY A CELEBRA-
TION OF LIFE AS IT IS A
RETURN TO THE TRIBAL.
UNION WITH NATURE
AND ONE ANOTHER,
NUDITY WITHOUT
SHAME, THE FORMING OF
A CIRCLE—ALL THESE
ARE WELL PROVEN
RITUAL DEVICES FOR
MULTIPLE BONDING AND
FOR EXPERIENCING THE
JOY OF BEING ALIVE AND
HUMAN.

not accompanied by the ingestion of psychotropic substances, ecstatic forms of dance, deep meditation, visualization techniques, nudity (possibly with body painting), fasting, ritual sexuality.

Although only a small group of people actually do try *all* of these things, the expression of the same tribal impulse can also be found outside of that circle and among people who do not even recognize their participation in this revival. One only needs to take a look at the beaches of Europe, the United States, and elsewhere to see how hundreds and thousands of contemporaries gratefully glory in their natural state—nudity—just as many tribal peoples around the world have done (and still do) whenever and wherever the climate allowed for it. One only needs to listen to contemporary popular music to find trance-inducing rhythms and beats that simply "make" people move. One only needs to look at the dance forms developed during the last decades—truly a far cry from the stiff and formal ways of dance that were fashionable in the times of our grandparents.

These days, many forms of dance and music come close to being trance-inducing. One of the subdivisions of house music has even been given the name "Trance." In addition, it is not simply the style of dancing that approaches or revives the nature of tribal dancing, but also another dimension. In those places and at those moments where all the elements are just right—the crowd, the music, the ambiance, the moon—something happens that goes beyond the merely individual experience. Suddenly, in the way of synergy, the participating individuals actually disappear and a concerted, coherent, and merged group is born, for however short a time. In those very moments, the tribal spirit is truly manifest and, just as in tribal societies, the dance becomes a release and a catharsis for the entire community.

Just as the new appreciation of nudity is winning ground from the idea that the body has to be hidden, and just as the new dances encourage people to shake all their flesh and bones rather than their legs only, so also have forgotten forms of sexuality arisen. Rather than copulating half dressed, with shame and the lights out, many women and men have learned that sexuality is the most beautiful and powerful expression of the life force—a knowledge that had been suppressed and almost forgotten during the last two millennia.

This particular expression of the tribal impulse started manifesting itself in what is now known as the sexual revolution of the 1960s but which, in fact, had already begun in the 1950s among members of the so-called Beat generation. The 1960s, however, aided by the new music and the influx of Eastern teachings, brought the first large-scale breakthrough in which the then prevailing culture of shame gave way to the then radical liberation in terms of human sexuality and gender-relationships. Although there is no reason at all to glorify this decade, because much in it was as immature as it was passionate and heartfelt, all subsequent developments are indebted to those who then started to experiment with what they thought of as "new" forms of sexual expression. Extended families, communes, multiple partner relationships, orgies: a long list of liberations from earlier dos and don'ts concerning homosexuality and promiscuity.

Considering that sexuality, next to the survival instinct, is the strongest of energies in all that is alive, it should come as no surprise that the tribal impulse manifests itself most strongly—and to many perhaps most shockingly—on this level. The very development in this area that started in the 1960s is still continuing. When we look at the social landscape with open and nonjudgmental eyes, we see today no less of a revolution; in fact, future sociologists may know it as the second sexual revolution, set in the explosive 1990s.

From the hundreds of Tantra workshops to the infamous dark rooms of party centers and nightclubs from Paris to New York to Amsterdam, people are redis-covering human sexuality as something altogether different than we have been led to think. The sexual impulse, as human history shows us abundantly, has little care for monogamous love relationships merely centered on the creation of new life. What we see in most civilizations, societies, cultures, or tribal groups of the non-Christian or pre-Christian past is the fact that sexuality was used not only for creating children but in other ways as well: relationships and lifestyles involving many lovers and also types of sexuality not based in relationships at all.

Whereas nude, erotic, or outright sexual encounters in the context of more than two people are often regarded today as strange or—depending on the inter-preter—even perverse expressions of an over-sexed hedonism, past generations often held a different view. What is and has been almost forgotten and/or sup-pressed is the fact that sexual activity with more than one partner, in the presence of others, or in mutual sharing, is a deep-rooted experience of humanity.

From caveman to late *Homo sapiens sapiens,* during a history of little change but the introduction of more and more technology and urban agglomeration, we have lived in close touch and in very close proximity to members of tribe, clan, and family; in caves, tents, brick houses, and tiny apartments; and often with promiscuity as a most usual and fully accepted behavioral standard.

In our genes as well as in our collective unconscious we carry a racial memory of a million nights of listening to—and often seeing—others make love, and of being watched and listened to ourselves. Consciously or unconsciously, we also remember the endless cycle of fertility festivals and other rites of life in which all of us—as our own ancestors—have taken part in hundreds or thousands of times. Our past lifestyles, at one time or another in many cultures and on all continents, have included situations in which three, four, ten, or hundreds of men and women have joined and mingled sexually and charged one another erotically, sharing love and desire, tension and trust, lust and pain, competition and friendship, existential aloneness and the warm sense of belonging.

Part of the motivation that makes some people want to be with others while erotically and sexually active is the wish to share—not necessarily one's partners but the very sense of love, pleasure, excitement, love, lust, trust, and abandon. The motivational and emotional spectrum of making love in the presence of others, and seeing others making love nearby, is wide. It contains elements of exhibitionism and voyeurism, but it also harks back to the deep memory of our species, which remembers and occasionally dreams up sexual group activities. Today, the many advertisements in which "couple seeks couple for erotic adventures" testify to a genetic memory that proves to be much stronger than any contemporary attempt at reprogramming humanity in the guise of so-called moral education.

Today's apparently new sexual practices, so beloved by tabloids thriving on the scandalous, range from sex with an unknown partner to sharing and exchanging partners to loving and/or living with more than one partner to the dark-room practices of the trendy gay and/or BDSM scene, which may be anonymous and public. All these expressions of the sexual impulse were well known to the ancients, from Greece to China and from India to South America.

Most ancient civilizations, being more fully cognizant of human nature, made room for such multiple, anonymous, public sexual activity from time to time, at least for a few days once a year.

Among the Romans, such a celebration was known as Floralia, an annual festival dedicated to the goddess Flora, during which the participants liberally enjoyed wine and sexual union, very much like the original carnivals of Western Europe and South America. At another time of the year, during the month of December, they celebrated the Saturnalia, an occasion dedicated to the deities of the harvest and marked by much sexual revelry. During the seven consecutive days of this festival, all social norms, differences of class, and sexual restrictions were abandoned, and all participants surrendered to the joy of freedom and of life.

In China, something very similar was known as the Web of Heaven and Earth, a fertility-oriented celebration intended to bring about an abundant harvest and the fertility of livestock. An auspicious night would be chosen with the help of oracular priests, and hundreds of men and women would meet in the fields in a general orgy under the open sky.

In India, the mythology of Krishna and the gopis (cowgirls) gave rise to the practice in which five, six, or seven women joined in sexual play with a single man—a practice apparently common enough to warrant specific terms for it in the Indian language: *pancha chakra* (five women) or *gopi chakra* (more than five). Whereas this practice seems to be mainly directed at the man's pleasure and related to the idea of a harem, the Greek equivalent certainly shows the women to be the active partners and very much in charge. The poor man who fell victim to the drugged and frenzied Maenads, priestesses of the wine-god, would usually not survive the orgy they made him part of.

In both Tibetan and Indian Tantra, things are much more ordered and ritualized. Here, the clearly stated aim is to arouse sexual energy by the combined efforts of several people in order to transcend the ego and the limited vision of everyday consciousness. In the Tibetan practice known as *zap-lam*, one woman is aided by two men to achieve the state known, in Western sexual magic, as erotocomatose lucidity: lucidity brought on by total sexual exhaustion. Involving many more players, Tantric couples in India often gathered in large groups to celebrate what is called *choli-marga*. With the women arriving before the men, each would drop a piece of her clothing into a basket from which the men would later pick one up, thus determining who would partner with whom during that night.

The above examples, selected from many more, will suffice to show how widespread and fully human such practices are, and they also show that such types of sexuality do not at all have to be at odds with religion and morals. It all depends on the set of morals employed and the degree of wisdom achieved by a given religion and society. Although it may seem that little can stop this trend toward more and more freedom of sexual expression, the opposition to it from the "moral majority" is understandably strong. What is strange about this opposition, a cynic might feel, is the fact that most of those moral people, whether Christian, Judaic, or Islamic, are the very ones who practice another very ancient and very tribal ritual and forcibly inflict it on every young boy: circumcision of the foreskin. By doing so, they in fact show themselves to celebrate pain and bloodletting rather than joy and sexuality.

Conclusion

THE IRRATIONAL TEMPTATION OF PASSING JUDGMENT

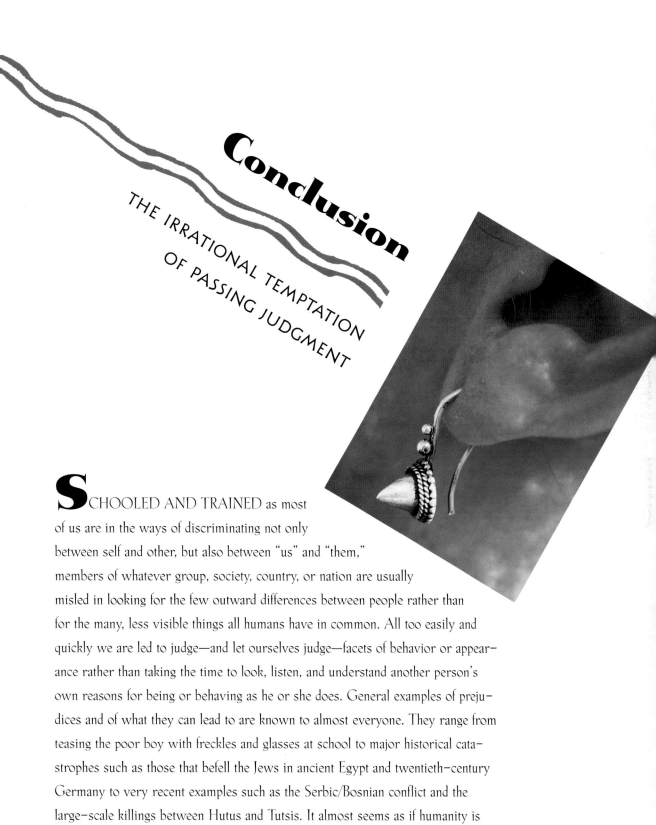

SCHOOLED AND TRAINED as most of us are in the ways of discriminating not only between self and other, but also between "us" and "them," members of whatever group, society, country, or nation are usually misled in looking for the few outward differences between people rather than for the many, less visible things all humans have in common. All too easily and quickly we are led to judge—and let ourselves judge—facets of behavior or appearance rather than taking the time to look, listen, and understand another person's own reasons for being or behaving as he or she does. General examples of prejudices and of what they can lead to are known to almost everyone. They range from teasing the poor boy with freckles and glasses at school to major historical catastrophes such as those that befell the Jews in ancient Egypt and twentieth-century Germany to very recent examples such as the Serbic/Bosnian conflict and the large-scale killings between Hutus and Tutsis. It almost seems as if humanity is not able to learn from even the painful experiences.

To return to the topic of this book, I have collected here a few examples of people's irrational temptation to pass judgment without looking first at the facts. Read them with an open mind and recognize not only your neighbor in them but yourself.

By far the most common piercing is one that most people do not even perceive as a piercing. One can easily meet a woman wearing one or two earrings who thinks that piercing is truly strange and that she personally would *never* do it. Previously reserved for women only—at least in the Western world—earrings have become very popular among men as well—since the 1960s.

An African visitor to present-day urban Germany was surprised and apparently slightly dismayed at seeing so many people with piercings. Told that he comes from a continent with a long history of doing just that, he exclaimed, "But that's African!" It was quite difficult to explain to him that here and now, *tribal* has become a concept dependent not on kinship or bloodline but on shared values.

A woman with artificially enlarged breasts and a facelift, meeting someone who wears a few piercings in lip or eyebrow, may easily judge herself as normal, but her fellow human as deviant.

A young French teenager with metal inserted in her eyebrows, nose, and lips finds it "absolutely crazy" that someone else would undergo surgery in order to put hair back on his bald head.

A young American, habitually circumcised like most of his unfortunate compatriots, thinks that scarification of a young African woman is something "forced" upon her by her traditional society. He also believes that such practices should be banned and does not see any connection between this and his own mutilation. During earlier centuries when the Roman Catholic Church encouraged the practice of having young boys castrated simply in order to make them better singers in the church's choirs, they saw no reason to condone other, even less severe forms of body modification or adornment.

Conclusion

Two contemporary men, one an army general and one the chief executive of a large banking corporation, call it "totally crazy" when seeing images of several tribal chiefs from Papua New Guinea in my collection. They refer to these men's type of dress, their painted bodies, and their elaborate headdresses prepared from bird feathers and bones stuck through their noses. They are completely unaware that others, looking at them, see an equally crazy sight. Fully dressed in dark colors, although it is high summer, and with their necks tightly tied by a tie and their feet sweating in boxes made from dead animals, they adhere equally to the local standard of their respective tribes: with his uniform and shining medals showing his valor in combat, and the executive with his false teeth and expensive watch shining brightly when he puts on a politician's smile.

Today, as we witness the widespread reemergence of the tribal impulses we've discussed in this book, the general tolerance for what people do with or to their own bodies is still lacking—but it is also slowly widening. To a large part, this process is aided by popular and thus influential artists, especially musicians, by other media stars such as fashion designers and photo models, and by the print and electronic media that carry their images and messages into the world. Combined, these artists and the media that cover them create what the artist formerly known as Prince once named a "sign of the times." Whereas he, finally and consequently, transformed himself into such a sign, becoming truly an icon, others created similar signs of their times in a more verbal manner.

The Beatles created, knowingly or not, a sort of new first commandment to a whole generation in the short sentence "All you need is love," just as a currently appreciated commandment is Madonna's "Express yourself."

Notwithstanding how different these statements may be, and how different the personalities that created them, they share one basic human concept that is all too often overlooked in the heat of the moment. What we all need in order to live together on this small planet, and what we need to express, is something as seemingly simple as respect: respect for each other's tastes, choices, wants, and needs. This includes respect for each other's visions of beauty, each other's ways to be sexually active, and each other's manners of body adornment, whether invisible or visible.

Glossary

Note: words set in **bold** indicate further references within this glossary

ABDOMINOPLASTY

Technical term in **cosmetic surgery** for what is better known as a tummy-tuck: a rather common form of body modification aimed at hiding the effects of aging and/or unhealthy habits. Although this and other practices of cosmetic surgery have nothing to do with a return to the tribal, but rather with the misplaced cult of youth, they do represent modern forms of body modification, of taking charge of one's own image.

ADHESIVE TATTOO

The removable adhesive or decal tattoo is, in fact, not a **tattoo** at all. Rather, it is simply a type of mass-market adornment that could perhaps be classified as a form of **makeup.** The best and most honest name for it would be fake tattoo, but such a name would not be conducive to sales.

BEADING

The insertion of small beads under the incised skin of the phallus, possibly as an attempt to make a small one bigger (or rather thicker) or to provide additional sensory stimulation to one's partner. The negative effect is that it looks much more like a dildo than the real thing.

BODY ADORNMENT

A generic term for a variety of techniques aimed at adorning or decorating one or more parts of the body more or less temporarily, either habitually or for special occasions. Although some

109

techniques of body adornment involve a certain degree of **body modification,** the two terms are not synonyms. Typical examples of body adornment are **body painting, makeup,** and **henna designs** on hands or feet. But the **cosmetic tattoo,** wearing earrings (with a **piercing** or not), and such "normal" things as coloring, shaving, or cultivating facial or other hair also belong to this category. In short, one can rightfully state that almost every human on the planet, with very few exceptions, engages in body adornment of one kind or another. Concerning **tattooing,** there seems to be no general consensus about whether it is a decoration or a modification. Clearly, a small tattoo on the arm or buttocks is very different from a neck or skull reshaped in early childhood. On the other hand, except for the cosmetic tattoo, the regular tattoo represents a permanent change of that part of one's skin and of one's overall appearance.

BODY DECORATION

See **Body Adornment.**

BODY MODIFICATION

A generic term for a variety of techniques aimed at changing one or more parts of the body from the natural state into a consciously designed state. Although techniques of body modification are sometimes used as a means of **body adornment** or decoration, the two terms are not synonyms. Among the ancient forms of modification we find, for example,

skull modeling, subincision, scarification, and enlarged **piercings,** with some of these techniques being revived in the present among modern people in both East and West. Truly modern forms of body modification are found in the form of the innumerable face-lifts, breast enlargements, hair replacements, and other techniques of **cosmetic surgery.** **Tattooing** is sometimes counted among the techniques of body modification, certainly in those cases where large parts of the body are thus made into a living work of art.

BODY PAINTING

In its most general sense, this term refers to all instances in which one or more parts of the body are artificially colored. Thus used, body painting embraces every kind of **makeup** from eyeliner, rouge, or henna designs for the hands and feet to the almost psychedelic look of a fully painted tribal chief from Papua New Guinea. During the last two or three decades, the term has become used in a more limited way. In this sense, which is also used in this book, body painting refers to coloring all or large portions of the nude human body.

BRANDING

A form of **scarification** usually achieved by burning the skin with heated metal. The practice has its roots in the branding of animals in order to mark them as property and, among humans, in slavery as it was known in Egypt, Rome, and elsewhere. Slaves were marked

---

KARO WOMAN

PAINTED AND RICHLY ADORNED WITH COWRIE SHELLS AND BEAD NECKLACES, THIS KARO BEAUTY ALSO WEARS A STICK OR PERHAPS A NAIL THROUGH HER PIERCED LOWER LIP. SIMILAR LIP INSERTS HAVE ALSO BEGUN TO APPEAR IN CONTEMPORARY CITIES, ALTHOUGH URBAN TRIBALS USUALLY WEAR SHORTER VERSIONS.

ROYAL HANDS, IN NINETEENTH-CENTURY VIETNAM

IN SEVERAL FAR EASTERN NATIONS, AMONG THEM CHINA AND THAILAND, IT WAS A WIDESPREAD CUSTOM AMONG WOMEN AND MEN TO GROW THE FINGERNAILS TO LENGTHS OF ABOUT FOUR CENTIMETERS—AT LEAST AMONG THOSE FOR WHOM MANUAL LABOR WAS NOT NECESSARY. HOWEVER, AS CAN BE SEEN IN THIS IMAGE FROM 1876, THE NOBILITY WENT MUCH FURTHER, WITH EACH CENTIMETER OF UNBROKEN NAIL GAINING THE WEARER A MORE EXALTED STATUS.

with nonremovable collars and often by branding them with a specific sign, for example, an *S* for *slave*. In other places, for example England and France, branding was used to mark criminals or heretics, a practice that continued up to the eighteenth century.

The same technique, fueled by a different motivation, has been applied in the United States in the twentieth century. Here, fraternity members, especially those with a predominantly black membership, have branded themselves in order to show their allegiance to the organization. As author Michelle Delio writes, "the practice continues to this day and many prominent figures, such as Chicago Bulls star Michael Jordan, Emmit Smith of the Dallas Cowboys, and the Reverend Jesse Jackson, have the Greek letters of their fraternities indelibly emblazoned into their skins."[21]

In yet another context, branding is sometimes used as perhaps the most radical sign of sexual submission and possession. It has been described, for example, in the famous novel *The Story of O*.

In recent years, however, people have begun to use branding as a means of adornment, choosing it along with or instead of **tattooing**. In several countries, even in the usually rather enlightened Netherlands, the practice of branding is banned by law. So far, it is still the rarest form of body adornment, but it is definitely on the rise.

CASTRATION

The surgical removal of a man's testicles, resulting in the loss of fertility and a hormonal imbalance that weakens male and strengthens female physical traits. In the long history of castration we encounter a variety of motivations for this practice: self-chosen (and sometimes self-inflicted) castration in order not to "sin," self-castration in order to please a deity, the punishment of criminals, a job requirement for harem guards and administrators, and the retention of an outstanding singing voice in a boys' choir.

CERVICOFACIAL RHYTIDECTOMY

Technical term in **cosmetic surgery** for what is better known as a face-lift; now a very

common form of body modification.

CIRCUMCISION

By circumcision we usually understand the cutting away of all or a part of the foreskin usually surrounding the glans penis, regardless of the individual or cultural motivation cited for this **body modification** or, as some call it, mutilation. Although this practice is often believed to be specifically Jewish and/or Islamic, evidence put forward by one of the world's foremost anthropologists predates these religions and goes back to the Old Stone Age.[22] Circumcision is one of the few practices of body modification that I'd like to see outlawed and discontinued. Sometimes one also speaks of female circumcision. However, considering that the degree of the modification involved, the loss of physical substance, and the loss of functionality are much greater in these cases, the various surgical practices are much better referred to as **clitoridectomy, infibulation,** or **labia removal.**

CLITORIDECTOMY

The terrible practice—not only painful and harmful, but also usually done without consent of the female—in which the visible part of the clitoris and parts of the labia are cut away, resulting in the loss of erotic/sexual feeling during masturbation or sexual play. It is one of the few practices of body modification that I'd like to see outlawed and discontinued.

See also **Labia Removal.**

COSMETIC SURGERY

A subdivision of **plastic surgery** and a generic term for a variety of surgical procedures unrelated to disease or health and motivated by the simple personal desire to look different. Although cosmetic surgery has been used as an aid to change one's legal identity, most people undergo the discomfort and pay the price simply in order to be more beautiful or attractive in their own and/or others' eyes. The term *cosmetic surgery* is usually reserved for surgically achieved changes in the shape and/or size of the nose, chin, lips, breasts, belly, buttocks, genitals, or other parts of the body. Although many people, including contemporary surgeons, may believe this practice to be a modern invention, the term could rightfully be used for several ancient and modern tribal practices as well, for example, **dental modification** or enlarged **piercings** into which lip-plates or ear-disks are then inserted. Such ancient tribal practices as **subincision** and **scarification** are also early forms of cosmetic surgery.

Among modern practices, the techniques most often applied are the face-lift, thigh lift, buttock lift, tummy tuck, liposuction, breast augmentation or reduction, eyelid surgery, rhinoplasty, and otoplasty. Although some of these procedures are called rejuvenative and are thus made to seem connected to health, they do not actually rejuvenate the body but simply make it appear rejuvenated. Although this and other practices of cosmetic surgery have nothing to do with a return to the tribal, but rather with the misplaced cult of youth, they do represent modern forms of body modification, of taking charge of one's own image.

COSMETIC TATTOO

Different from the usual **tattooing,** this relatively new technique inserts color into the outermost layer of the skin only, resulting in a temporary tattoo that lasts from three to five years on the face and four to six years on the body. Cosmetic tattoos are most often used to modify and enhance the size or direction of one's eyebrows or, for example, to add a "beauty spot." The technique is also known as **permanent makeup.**

CUTTING

A specific form of **scarification** that involves incising or slashing the skin. Sometimes the process is repeated over time in order to achieve deep and clearly visible marks; in other cases, the wound is kept open temporarily in order to create pronounced and visible scars.

Within the context of tribal cultures, such cutting was often performed as a therapeutic means of enabling one to come to terms with other, more psychic forms of pain, for example the loss of a partner, friend, or relative. Although such usage and motivation are sometimes found among twentieth-century neotribals as well, the main reasons for being "cut" today seem to be **body adornment** and decoration (going a step further than tattooing) and/or the experience and endurance of the associated pain and the resulting respect one earns with that particular subculture. This latter motivation, again, is one known to tribal peoples around the world.

DECAL TATTOO
See **Adhesive Tattoo.**

DENTAL MODIFICATION
Various practices are known in which the hardest material of the human body is manipulated and modified. Whereas some tribal people simply color their teeth—a temporary decoration and simply a specialized form of makeup—others are much more radical in their approach. Practices include having the frontal teeth inlaid with gold and precious stones, filing or chipping the teeth until they become sharp points, and removing several or all teeth. A modern equivalent of these ancient forms of body modification are teeth visibly made from gold—a favorite practice in Turkey and other Near Eastern countries.

FINGER SACRIFICE
Whereas, among some peoples, one may slash one's arm, chest, or thigh (see **scarification**) in reaction to the death of a loved one—a pain never forgotten and a wound forever visible—other cultures and subcultures have resorted to the complete amputation of a finger in response to a personal failing the results of which one can never hope to set right. Among the Yakuza, members of Japan's centuries-old criminal underworld, the sacrifice of a finger is—short of ritual suicide—the only means of showing that one understands the true gravity of one's failing and that one takes full responsibility. Translated into modern European or American life, this would mean that a drunk driver who killed or maimed someone's child would call on the parents and, very formally

and in their presence, cut off his own pinky (if still available) and present it to his hosts as a token of his guilt and as a means of regaining his honor in their eyes.

FOOT-MODELING
Also known as foot-binding, this practice has been followed mainly in China and only on women. Although much has been made of the so-called golden lotus as a sign of beauty, it is ultimately an expression of male possessiveness. A woman with such deformed feet, stunted in their natural growth, is less likely to flee the possibly unsolicited advances of her husband, or at least is less able to take a strong physical stance.

HENNA DESIGNS
Somewhere between the practice of body adornment with ash, paint, or makeup (temporary) and the tattoo (permanent) are the designs created with henna. Usually applied to hands or feet, henna paste creates intricate, tattoo-like designs that stay visible for about two to four weeks.

INFIBULATION
Term for the terrible practice—not only painful and harmful, but also usually done without consent of the female—in which the labia are cut away and the edges of the wound are sewn together, simply in order to ensure that the girl/young woman may not engage in sexual intercourse. It is one of the few practices of body modification I'd like to see outlawed and discontinued.

LABIA ENLARGEMENT
The labia, especially the small, inner ones, not only are adorned by means of **piercing** but are also enlarged in some tribal cutures. Among the Hottentot people, a woman was judged beautiful and powerful if she had large inner labia extending far beyond the outer ones. They are purposely elongated and have been reported to be very large indeed. Early ethnologists called this the Hottentot apron. Other African tribes, such as the Urua of Central Africa, also practice(d) such artificial enlargement of the inner labia. As with all other practices of body modification, this one

has begun to return within certain modern subcultures.

LABIA LIFT
One of the newest practices to arrive is the labia lift. For the price of approximately $3,000, cosmetic surgeons will perform **liposuction** on the outer labia. The aim of thus reducing the fatty tissue is not merely to make the outer labia smaller but to render them more sensitive to stimulation. It seems, according to the first reports of women who have had this done, that orgasms not only are sweeter but occur more easily and frequently.

LABIA REMOVAL
Whereas more and more women have their labia or other parts of the genitals pierced and adorned, and others even enlarge their labia, there are again others—on the far side of the spectrum—who have these sensitive inner labia surgically removed because they are thought to be "too long," "too big," or otherwise "abnormal" rather than simply unique and special. However, at least in these cases the girl or woman in question does undergo such surgery at her own request. A quite different situation is found in some cultures, mainly in Africa, where **clitoridectomy** and/or **infibulation** are inflicted upon girls as a rule and often by force.

LIPOSUCTION
A technique of **cosmetic surgery** in which certain parts of the body are modified by the removal of "diet-resistant" fat. Most often applied to belly, buttocks, thighs, or neck.

MAKEUP
A general term for a variety of methods employed to change, highlight, or hide certain features of the body, most often the face. What is regarded as accepted and thus proper makeup changes from time to time, as fashion does, and certainly from society to society. Seen from a broad perspective, makeup is, in fact, a specialized form of body painting, ranging from applying rouge and lipstick to one's nipples (sixteenth-century France) to coloring one's fingernails (with nail polish or

henna) and covering one's lips, eyelids, and cheeks with colored powders or creams. Within the last decade, a mild form of **tattooing** has arrived in the beauty parlors of most contemporary societies. This **cosmetic tattoo** is also called **permanent makeup** in an attempt to avoid the stigma that has surrounded tattooing in most modern Western societies.

MODERN PRIMITIVE(S)

Modern primitive is a label applied to the recent revival of so-called primitive body modification practices. The term was coined in 1977 by Fakir Musafar, a modern Western experiential pioneer of many tribal modification techniques and commonly regarded as one of the major advocates and spokesmen of their revival, especially of the spiritual dimensions of the pain thus suffered. *Modern Primitives* is the title of a book, published in 1989, that contributed greatly to the further and widespread resurgence and acceptance of these tribal practices such as piercing, scarification, and tattooing.

NECK-MODELING

Rare among tribal people and not yet signaled among contemporary neotribals, neck modeling is a technique in which elongation of the neck is achieved by wearing metal rings around the neck, commencing in early childhood. The practice has been known in Africa as well but has survived only among the women of the Chin, a tribal people living in the border region between today's Myanmar (Burma) and Thailand. The longer one's neck, the higher one's status.

OTOPLASTY

Name for a technique of **cosmetic surgery** in which the ear is surgically remodeled and thus modified.

PERMANENT MAKEUP

See **Cosmetic Tattoo.**

PIERCING

Perforation of the skin and underlying tissue in order to create a small tunnel in one's skin and flesh, usually in a protruding portion of the earlobes, nostrils, nasal septum, lips, eyebrows, nipples, genitals, etc. As long as such a piercing is not enlarged by a weight or other means of dilation, it is a rather temporary body modification in the sense that once the inserted object is removed, the skin usually closes with time. Once sufficient enlargement of the originally small piercing has taken place by the insertion of such objects as metal rings, tubes, sticks and/or successively heavier weights, the piercing then becomes permanent. The type of piercing meant for insertion of rings, into whatever part of the body, is sometimes called ringing.

PLASTIC SURGERY

Based on the Greek *plastica* ("to mold" or "to form"), the term refers to surgical techniques aimed at reconstructing lost parts of the body, restoring function, or correcting acquired and/or congenital deformities (or whatever is defined as such). By its very nature, the age of plastic surgery cannot be archaeologically proved, yet the first documents attesting to its use come from the Indian subcontinent of about 200 B.C.E. and from the Italy of the Renaissance (fourteenth to sixteenth century). The advanced medical insights and technologies of the twentieth century, in conjunction with the innumerable wounded victims of World Wars I and II, gave rise to the variety of techniques available today. In their wake arose the well-publicized subdivision of plastic surgery generally known as **cosmetic surgery,** a now widely used and accepted manner of body modification.

RECONSTRUCTIVE SURGERY

See **Plastic Surgery.**

RHINOPLASTY

Name for a technique of **cosmetic surgery** in which the nose is surgically remodeled and thus modified.

RINGING

See **Piercing.**

SCARIFICATION

In a scientific sense, this term refers to the creation, by whatever technique, of one or more permanent scars on any part of the skin not by an accident or health-related surgery but by a conscious decision. Today, this decision is usually taken by the person to be thus decorated; yet, in centuries past the decision was often taken by someone in authority without the consent of the subject. In this sense, scarification includes several techniques, each of which leads to a different result or look: **branding,** simple **cutting,** and the types of cutting after which certain substances are introduced into the skin. In modern usage, within contemporary tattoo and piercing studios, the term *scarification* is often reserved for the latter method. In this sense, scarification involves cutting or incising the skin and then manipulating the cicatrization process by introducing ink, ashes, or other substances into the still open wound. Once these wounds heal, they leave more or less pronounced scars. The visual and tactile results achieved with this type of scarification are dependent on the cutting technique and the substance(s) introduced into the wound. Whether or not the wound results in a raised scar, a keloid, largely depends on the person's genetic heritage and on the amounts of melanocyte-stimulating hormone produced by the intermediate pituitary gland and of melatonin secreted by the pineal gland.

SKULL-MODELING

An ancient practice known in Egypt and China, especially within royal families and among the aristocracy, and also in Africa and Melanesia as well as among Native Americans such as the Chinook and the Kwakiutl. During the first few months of a child's life, his or her skull is artificially shaped so as to become elongated. Various peoples have used various means to achieve this but with similar motives. A high or long skull is meant to indicate heightened wisdom and/or intelligence, apart from showing the person's high-born status. Also known as *skull-shaping.*

SUBINCISION

A practice mainly known from the initiation ceremonies and puberty rites of Australian Aborigines. By slitting open the underside of the phallus along the whole length of the urethra, a man simulates having a vulva. The motivation seems to be a need to acquire some of the female magic of periodic bleeding, to which end a man will again and again reopen the wound during strictly guarded ceremonies that no woman may ever attend. The initiated and subincised men are called "possessors of a vulva," and they are known to have sexual relations with young men not yet incised this way. Interestingly, there is no form of genital modification or mutilation for women among Australia's tribal people; such practices seem to be the sole preserve of male-dominated societies.

TATTOOING

A widely practiced method of **body decoration** and/or **body modification** in which markings such as signs, symbols, and letters are applied to the body by puncturing the skin's outer layers and inserting color into it. Whether ancient or modern techniques are used, the skin is punctured with a sharp instrument, now usually an electric needle. In earlier times and other cultures, tattooing required one or more needles fixed to a stick and driven into the skin by slight hammering, the very process that has led to the term *tattoo* via the Polynesian sound-equivalent of the action: *tau tau.* The practice of tattooing is, and has always been, a worldwide phenomenon yet has been temporarily outlawed in a variety of societies, mainly those based on Judeo-Christian codes of behavior. Even today, where the tattoo has "gone mainstream" once more and tattooed people can be found in all walks of life, the practice is still illegal and/or restricted to persons over eighteen years of age in some states of the United States.

Endnotes

1. Marshall McLuhan, *The Medium is the Massage*, p. 63.

2. Love, *Encylopedia of Unusual Sexual Practices*, p. 61.

3. Campbell, *Primitive Mythology*, p. 423.

4. Ibid., p. 211.

5. Martischnig, *Tätowierung ostasiastischer Art*, p. 8.

6. Ibid., pp. 11–12.

7. Ibid., p. 22.

8. Lazi, *The Tattoo*, pp. 21–23.

9. Brain, *The Decorated Body*, p. 90.

10. Lazi, p. 24.

11. Califia, *Public Sex*, p. 232.

12. Levi-Strauss, Claude, *The Raw and the Cooked*.

13. In 1996, in the *Body Modification Enzine* (the "extreme" section with limited access). <http://www.bme.freq.com>

14. Lawlor, *Voices of the First Day*, p. 344.

15. Fraser, *The Golden Bough*, p. 180.

16. Schiffmacher, *1000 Tattoos*, p. 9.

17. From an interview of Tom and Shannon by Raven Rowanchilde.

18. Metzger, *The Woman Who Slept with Men to Keep the War Out of Them and Tree*, p. 219.

19. Watson, *Gifts of Unknown Things*, pp. 52–61.

20. From *PFIQ (Piercing Fans International Quarterly)* no. 47, pp. 30–32.

21. Michelle Delio, "Playing with Fire: Body Branding," originally published in *Tattoo Savage* magazine (n.d.), then published on the Internet.

22. Ashley Montague, "Mutilated Humanity," *The Humanist*, vol. 55, July 1, 1995, p. 12.

Bibliography

NONFICTION BOOKS

Becchetti, Catherine. *Le mystère dans les lettres*. Bangkok: Editions des cahiers de France, 1991.

Beckwith, Carol, and Angela Fisher. *African Ark*. London: Collins Harvill, 1990.

Beckwith, Carol, and Angela Fisher. *Women of the African Ark*. San Francisco: Pomegranate Artbooks, 1993.

Berman, Morris. *Coming to Our Senses: Body and Spirit in the Hidden History of the West*. New York: Simon & Schuster, 1989.

Berns, Marla C. "Ga'anda Scarification: A Model for Art and Identity" (in Rubin, *Marks of Civilization*).

Bianchi, Robert S. "Tattoo in Ancient Egypt" (in Rubin, *Marks of Civilization*).

Blacking, John (ed.). *The Anthropology of the Body*. London: Academic Press, 1978.

Bohannan, Paul. "Beauty and Scarification Amongst the Tiv" (in Rubin, *Marks of Civilization*).

Brain, Robert. *The Decorated Body*. New York: Harper & Row, 1979.

Briffault, Robert. *The Mothers: A Study of the Origins of Sentiments and Institutions* (3 Vols.). London: Allen & Unwin, 1927.

Buckley, Thomas, and Alma Gottlieb (eds.). *Blood Magic: The Anthropology of Menstruation*. Berkeley: Univiversity of California Press, 1988.

Cohen, Tony. *The Tattoo*. Sidney: Adrian Savvas Publishing, 1994.

Daniels, Ger. *Volksversieringen uit alle werelddelen* (Folk-Decorations Around the Globe). Antwerpen, Belgium: Uitgeverij C. de Vries-Brouwers, 1989.

Davidson, Basil. *Africa: History of a Continent*. New York: Spring Books, 1972.

Delio, Michelle. *Tattoo: Lichaamskunst als spiegel van de ziel*. Alphen an den Rijn: Atrium, 1994. (English edition: Carlton Books, 1993.)

DeMichele, William. *The Illustrated Woman*. New York: Proteus Press, 1992.

Duerr, Hans Peter. *Nacktheit und Scham: Der Mythos vom Zivilisationsprozeß*, Vol. 1. Frankfurt: Suhrkamp Taschenbuch Verlag, 1994.

Duerr, Hans Peter. *Intimität: Der Mythos vom Zivilisationsprozeß*, Vol. 2. Frankfurt: Suhrkamp Taschenbuch Verlag, 1994.

Duerr, Hans Peter. *Obszönität und Gewalt: Der Mythos vom Zivilisationsprozeß*, Vol. 3. Frankfurt: Suhrkamp Taschenbuch Verlag, 1995.

Ebin, Victoria. *The Body Decorated*. London: Thames & Hudson, 1979.

Eliade, Mircea. *Rites and Symbols of Initiation*. San Francisco: Harper & Row, 1975.

Fisher, Angela. *Africa Adorned*. London: Collins Harvill, 1994.

Fraser, James G. *The Golden Bough: A Study in Magic and Religion*. New York: Macmillan, 1987.

Gibson, William. *Burning Chrome*. London: Grafton, 1988.

———. *Count Zero*. New York: Ace, 1987.

———. *Mona Lisa Overdrive*. London: Grafton, 1990.

———. *Neuromancer*. London: Grafton, 1986.

Gluckman, Max (ed.). *Essays on Rituals of Social Relations*. Manchester: Manchester University Press, 1962.

Grognard, Catherine, and Claudio Lazi. *The Tattoo: Graffiti for the Soul*. London: Sunburst Books, 1994.

Handy, W. *Tattooing in the Marquesas*. Bulletin of the Bernice P. Bishop Museum, 1922.

Harrer, Heinrich. *De laatste 500: Een expeditie naar de dwergvolken van de Andamanen* (The Last 500: An Expedition to the Andaman Islands). Rijswijk, The Netherlands: Elmar, 1979.

Harris, Marvin. *Cultural Anthropology*. New York: HarperCollins, 1995.

Hartsuiker, Dolf. *Sadhus: Holy Men of India*. London: Thames & Hudson, 1993.

Kirk, Malcolm. *Man As Art: New Guinea* (with an Essay by Andrew Strathern). San Francisco: Chronicle Books, 1993.

Lawlor, Robert. *Voices of the First Day: Awakening in the Aboriginal Dreamtime*. Rochester, Vt.: Inner Traditions International, 1991.

Levins, Hoag. *American Sex Machines: The Hidden History of Sex at the U.S. Patent Office*. Holbrook, Mass.: Adams Media Corporation, 1996.

Levi-Strauss, Claude. *The Raw and the Cooked*. Chicago: University of Chicago Press, 1969.

Loth, Heinrich. *Die Frau im alten Afrika* (Woman in Ancient Africa). Leipzig: Edition Leipzig, 1986.

Love, Brenda. *The Encyclopedia of Unusual Sex Practices*. Fort Lee, N.J.: Barricade Books, 1992.

Majupuria, Indra. *Nepalese Women*. Kathmandu: M. Devi, 1982.

Mallery, Garrick. *Picture Writing of the American Indians*. New York: Dover, 1972.

Marcus, Greil. *Lipstick Traces: A Secret History of the Twentieth Century*. Cambridge: Harvard University Press, 1989.

Martischnig, Michael. *Tätowierung ostasiatischer Art* (Tattooing the East-Asian Way). Vienna: Akademie der Wissenschaften, 1987.

McCallum, Donald. "Historical and Cultural Dimensions of the Tattoo in Japan" (in Rubin, *Marks of Civilization*).

McLuhan, Marshall. *The Medium is the Massage*. New York: Bantam, 1967.

———. *Understanding Media: Extension of Man*. New York: Signet, 1966.

Metzger, Deena. *The Woman Who Slept With Men to Keep the War Out of Them and Tree*. Berkeley, CA: Wingbow Press, 1988.

Oettermann, Stephan. *Zeichen auf der Haut: Die Geschichte der Tätowierung in Europa* (The European History of the Tattoo). Hamburg: Europäische Verlagsanstalt, 1994.

Reitzenstein, F. von. *Das Weib bei den Naturvölkern* (Woman Among Tribal Peoples). Berlin: Neufeld & Henius, no date (circa 1920).

Ricciardi, Mirella. *Vanishing Amazon*. London: Weidenfeld & Nicolson, 1991.

Richie, Donald, and Ian Buruma. *The Japanese Tattoo*. New York: Weatherhill, 1980.

Richter, Stefan. *Hidden Exposures*. Dordrecht, Netherlands: De Vaar, 1994.

Roberts, Allen F. "Tabwa Tegumentary Inscription" (in Rubin, Marks of Civilization).

Rosen, Michael A. *Sexual Portraits: Photographs of Radical Sexuality*. San Francisco: Shaynew Press, 1990.

———. *Sexual Art: Photographs That Test the Limits*. San Francisco: Shaynew Press, 1994.

Rubin, Arnold. *Marks of Civilization: Artistic Transformations of the Human Body*. Los Angeles: Museum of Cultural History, 1988.

———. "Tattoo Trends in Gujarat" (in Rubin, *Marks of Civilization*).

Saitoti, Tepilit Ole, and Carol Beckwith. *Maasai*. New York: Harry N. Abrams, 1993.

Sanders, Clinton R. *Customizing the Body: The Art and Culture of Tattooing*. Philadelphia: Temple University Press, 1989.

Schiffmacher, Henk. *1000 Tattoos*. Cologne: Benedikt Taschen Verlag, 1996.

Sinha, Indra. *The Great Book of Tantra: Translations and Images from the Classic Indian Texts*. Rochester, Vt.: Inner Traditions, 1993.

Strathern, Andrew, and Marilyn Strattern. *Self-Decoration in Mount Hagen (Papua New Guinea)*. London: Gerald Duckworth & Co., 1971.

Bibliography

Teilhet-Fisk, Jehanne. "The Spiritual Significance of Newar Tattoos" (in Rubin, *Marks of Civilization*).

Thevoz, Michel. *Der bemalte Körper* (The Painted Body). Zurich: ABC Verlag, 1985.

Tilroe, Anna. *De huid van de kameleon: Over hedendaagse beeldende kunst* (The Skin of the Chameleon: About Contemporary Art). Amsterdam: Querido, 1996.

Turner, Victor. "Three Symbols of Passage in Ndembu Circumcision Ritual" (in Gluckman, ed., *Essays on Rituals of Social Relations*).

Vale, V., and Andrea Juno. *Modern Primitives: Tattoo—Piercing—Scarification*. San Francisco: Re/Search, 1989.

Verswijer, Gustaaf. *Mekreanoti: Living among the Painted People of the Amazon*. New York: Prestel, 1996.

Virel, Andre. *Decorated Man: The Human Body as Art*. New York: Harry N. Abrams, 1980.

Vogel, Susan. "Baule Scarification: The Mark of Civilization" (in Rubin, *Marks of Civilization*).

Watson, Lyall. *Gifts of Unknown Things*. Rochester, Vt.: Destiny Books, 1991.

Wojcik, Daniel. *Punk and Neo-Tribal Body Art*. Jackson: University Press of Mississipi, 1995.

Wolter, Jürgen. *Intim-Schmuck für Sie und Ihn*. Flensburg, Germany: Verlag Horst Dieter Adler, 1991.

Wroblewski, Chris. *Tattoed Women*. London: Virgin Publishing, 1992.

Ziegler-Zoschke. *Bodypiercing*. Vienna: Paul Zolnay Verlag, 1995.

MAGAZINE ARTICLES

"Baaba." *PFIQ* (Piercing Fans International Quarterly), 47, April 1996.

Edger and Dingman. "Tattooing and Identity." *International Journal of Social Psychiatry*, 1963.

"The Labia Lift." Short item in the Dutch edition of *Marie Claire*, September 1996, p. 29.

Leland, John. "Welcome to the Jungle." *Newsweek*, September 23, 1991 pp. 53–54.

Menkes, Suzy. "Fetish or Fashion?" *New York Times*, November 24, 1993.

Phillipps, W. J. "An Introduction to the Study of Tattooing Chisels of the Maori with Notes on Tattoo." *Dominion Records in Ethnology*, Vol. 1, No. 3, 1948.

Rowanchilde, Raven. "Tom and Shannon" in *Urban Primitive: Transformation in the Urban Jungle*. 1995, 1996, 1997. < http://www.clo.com/~raven/ > (25 May 1997).

Smeaton, W. "Tattooing Among the Arabs of Iraq." *American Anthropologist*, Vol. 39, 1937.

Turner, Terence. "Tchikrin: A Central Brazilian Tribe and its Symbolic Language of Bodily Adornment." *Natural History*, Vol. 78, 1969.

BODY DECORATION IN FICTION

Califia, Pat. *Macho Sluts*. Boston: Alyson Publications, 1988.

Fisher, Sarah. *The Contract*. Leed, Great Britain: Silver Mink, 1996.

Heller, Marcus van. *Roman Orgy*. London: Nexus, 1989.

Joanou, Alice. *Tourniquet*. New York: Masquerade, 1992.

Matheson, Richard C. *Scars and Other Distinguishing Marks*. New York: Tor, 1988.

Nin, Anais. *Delta of Venus*. London: Star, 1978.

Reage, Pauline (Dominique Aury). *The Story of O* (1954). New York: Ball, 1990.

Tanizaki, Junichiro. *Shisei* (The Tattooer). 1910.

VIDEOTAPES AND FILMS

For information concerning videotapes of Cindy Jackson's transformation, send a self-addressed envelope to Cindy Jackson, P.O. Box 3410, Highgate, London N6 4EE, United Kingdom.

The "Hole" Experience. Prince of Pain Productions, Body Basics, 613 Briar, Dept. OB, Chicago, IL 60657.

Mistress of the Rings (VHS). 25-minute video on the art of body piercing, featuring Mette Hintze of the Black Universe in Copenhagen, who talks about and demonstrates piercings, from earlobes to genitals. Det Dansk Filmvaerksted, Steen Shapiro and Anne Marie Kuerstein. Versterbragade 24, DK-1620 Copenhagen V, Denmark. (45) 3124-1624, fax: (45) 3124-4419

Piercing with a Pro Video Series (VHS, PAL, BETA) 1: The 9 Traditional Male Piercings, $69.95; 2: The Female and Unisex Piercings, $49.95 plus postage. Available through Gauntlet catalog (see *PFIQ* entry below).

Piercing Nipples (VHS). Pleasurable Piercings, Inc., $39.95 plus postage. Pleasurable Piercings, 7 Garfield Ave., Hawthorne, NJ 07506. (201) 779-2782. Navel, nostril, septum piercing. Videos available soon.

Pierced and Painted (VHS). 75 minutes of tattooing and piercing: "explicit scenes of body tattooing, full frontal nudity, and actual genital piercing." (800) 748-7853.

Wildcat International Videos (PAL, VHS), 16 Preston St., Brighton, BN1 2HN England, (0273) 323758. Wildcat offers a very wide selection of videos, mostly "show-off" collections featuring heavily/uniquely pierced and inked men and women. Contact Wildcat for catalog and availability.

MAGAZINES

Body Art. Publications Limited, P.O. Box 32, Great Yarmouth, Norfolk, NR29 5RD, England. Body Art imposes self-censorship to stay on the legal side of the rigid obscenity laws. It shows body modifications for anthropological and decorative purposes, not for sexual purposes, and does not show the same level of explicit material as in *PFIQ*.

Body Play and Modern Primitives Quarterly. Insight Books, P.O. Box 2575, Menlo Park, CA 94026-2575 U.S.A. This publication is produced by Fakir Musafar.

Erotic Passion. Published by Creative Art Collection, Postfach 1317, L-1013 Luxembourg. Distributed in Germany by ZBF-Vertriebs GmbH, Schlossbergstrasse 23, D-6200 Weisbaden / Schierstein.

Intim-Schmuck. Barnas Verlag Landrat von Laer Str. 17-19 D 47495 Rheinberg, Germany.

Flesh Canvas. Rodan Publishing, P.O. Box 139B, East Molesey, Surrey KT8 9YQ England, (081) 941-7580, fax (081) 941-7582. Equal coverage of tattoos and piercings, with photographs of the piercing process.

In The Flesh. Published semiannually by OB Enterprises, Inc., Suite 2305, 450 Seventh Ave., New York, NY 10123-0101, U.S.A.

(PFIQ) Piercing Fans International Quarterly. Gauntlet, Inc., 2215-R Market St., Suite 801, San Francisco, CA 94114. Write for order form; signature and declaration of 21+ age required.

Piercing World. Published by P.A.U.K., 153 Tomkinson Rd., Nuneaton, Warwickshire, CV10 8DP, England. Quarterly, full-color publication. Annual subscription: pounds 16 UK, pounds 20 Europe, pounds 25 overseas. Subscription to *Piercing World* brings automatic membership in P.A.U.K. Detailed color and black-and-white photos of piercings and tattoos, unusual jewelry designs, multiple piercings, and piercing techniques, including all genital piercings. The magazine also includes a classified ads section and a list of EPPA-registered piercers. *Piercing World* is also available through Pleasurable Piercings, 7 Garfield Ave., Hawthorne, NJ 07506.

Tattoo Savage. Published quarterly by Paisano Publications, Inc. Subscriptions: P.O. Box 469062, Escondido, CA 92046-9062. (619) 738-8907.

Illustration Credits

p. ii: Photograph © William DeMichele 1997 from the book *The Illustrated Woman*, Proteus Press

p. vi: © Gilles Frenke

p. 1: Photograph © Rufus C. Camphausen

p. 3: © Karo

p. 4 top: Photograph © Carol Beckwith & Angela Fisher

p. 4 bottom: Photograph © Darrel N. T. Tsen

p. 7 top: Photograph © Angela Fisher

p. 7 bottom: Photograph © William DeMichele 1997 from the book *The Illustrated Woman*, Proteus Press

p. 8 top: Photograph © Meg Kukta

p. 8 bottom: Photograph © Carol Beckwith & Angela Fisher

p. 12 top: Photograph © Gustaaf Verswijver

p. 12 middle: Photograph © Spring Cerise

p. 12 bottom: Photograph © Charles & Josette Lenars

p. 14: Photograph of Peri Wyrrd © Meghan Scanlon

p. 15: Photograph © Carol Beckwith & Angela Fisher

p. 17 top: Photograph © Photo J. Faris

p. 17 bottom: "Sun Goddess back." Photograph of Elizabeth Knock © Natasha von Rosenschilde

p. 20 top: Photograph © Claudio Lazi

p. 20 bottom: Photograph © Corrie A. Bos

p. 21 top: Photograph © George Zaloumis

p. 21 middle: Photograph © Carol Beckwith & Angela Fisher

p. 21 bottom: Photograph © Meghan Scanlon

p. 24: Photograph © Klaus C. Meyer/Black Star

p. 25: "Snake Goddess with Egg and Dove," detail. Photograph of Danielle © Natasha von Rosenschilde

p. 27 top: Photograph © Frank van Paridon

p. 27 bottom: Photograph © Carol Beckwith & Angela Fisher

p. 29 top: Photograph © Angela Fisher

p. 29 middle: Photograph © Susan McCartney/Photograph Researchers Inc.

p. 29 bottom: Photograph © Carol Beckwith & Angela Fisher

p. 30 top: Photograph © Angela Fisher

p. 30 bottom: Photograph courtesy of the Royal Geographic Society

p. 31 top: Photograph © Charles & Josette Lenars

p. 31 bottom: Photograph © Charles & Josette Lenars

p. 32 top: Photograph © V. Lazonga

p. 32 middle: Photograph © Rufus C. Camphausen

p. 32 bottom: Photograph © Rufus C. Camphausen

p. 34 top: Photograph by Todd Friedman © 1997 www.TFPhoto.com

p. 34 bottom: Photograph © Gustaaf Verswijver

p. 35 top: Photograph © Stefan Richter 1997. All rights reserved.

p. 35 bottom: Photograph © M. Folco/Black Star

p. 36: "Scorpio Angel back." Photograph of James © Natasha von Rosenschilde

p. 37: Photograph © Angela Fisher

p. 40 top: Photograph © Chris Wroblewski

p. 40 bottom: Photograph courtesy of Haddon College, Cambridge

p. 41 top: Photograph © Charles & Josette Lenars

p. 41 bottom: Photograph © Angela Fisher

p. 43 top: Photograph of Peri Wyrrd © Vatsala Sperling

p. 43 bottom: Photograph © P. Brahm (Zefa)

p. 44 top: Photograph © Angela Fisher

p. 44 bottom: Photograph © Mirella Ricciardi

p. 45 top: Photograph © Peter Bennetts

p. 45 bottom: Photograph © Mirella Ricciardi

p. 46 top: Photograph © Christina Camphausen

p. 46 middle: Photograph © Rufus C. Camphausen

p. 46 bottom: Photograph © Marcos Joly

p. 49 top: Photograph © Maureen Bisilliat

p. 49 bottom: Photograph © Gustaaf Verswijver

p. 50 top: "Female Falcon Wind Angel." Photograph of Kateri Walker © Natasha von Rosenschilde

p. 50 bottom: Photograph © David Hancock/Skyscans

p. 51 top: Photograph © Carol Beckwith & Angela Fisher

p. 51 bottom: Photograph © Carol Beckwith & Angela Fisher

p. 52 top: Photograph © Peter Bennetts

p. 52 bottom: Photograph © Angela Fisher

p. 53 top: Photograph © Charles & Josette Lenars

p. 53 bottom: Photograph © Peter Bennetts

p. 54 top: Photograph © Carol Beckwith & Angela Fisher

p. 54 bottom: Photograph © Charles & Josette Lenars

p. 56: Photograph © Richard Todd

p. 57: Photograph © S. Weir

p. 59 top: Photograph from the collection of the Amsterdam Tattoo Museum

p. 59 bottom: Photograph © Rufus C. Camphausen

p. 61 top: Photograph © Charles & Josette Lenars

p. 61 middle: Photograph © Rob Webster

p. 61 bottom: Photograph © Charles & Josette Lenars

p. 62 top: Photograph from the collection of the Amsterdam Tattoo Museum

p. 62 bottom: Photograph from the collection of the Amsterdam Tattoo Museum

p. 63 top left: Photograph by S. Kinoshita Shiraoi

p. 63 top right: Photograph © Chris Wroblewski from the collection of Bob Maddison

p. 63 bottom: Copyright by Quantity Postcards, San Francisco

p. 66 top: Photograph © Rufus C. Camphausen

p. 66 bottom: Photograph © Angela Fisher

p. 67 top: Photograph © Rufus C. Camphausen

p. 67 bottom: Drawing © Ger Daniels

p. 68 top: Photograph by Todd Friedman © 1997 www.TFPhoto.com

p. 68 bottom: Photograph © Annie Sprinkle

p. 69 top: Photograph © Stefan Richter 1997. All rights reserved.

p. 69 bottom: Photograph © Rufus C. Camphausen

p. 70 top: © Mother Productions

p. 70 bottom: Photograph © Hella Hammid

p. 71: Photograph © Christina Camphausen

p. 72: Photograph © Carol Beckwith & Angela Fisher

p. 73: Photograph © Michael Müller

p. 75 top: Photograph by Todd Friedman © 1997 www.TFPhoto.com

p. 75 bottom: Photograph © Carol Beckwith & Angela Fisher

p. 76 top: Photograph © Carol Beckwith & Angela Fisher

p. 76 bottom: Photograph © William DeMichele 1997 from the book *The Illustrated Woman*, Proteus Press

p. 78 top: Photograph © Carol Beckwith & Angela Fisher

p. 78 bottom: Photograph © Johnnie Eisen

p. 80 top: © L. Zander

p. 80 middle: Drawing © Christina Camphausen

p. 80 bottom: Photograph © Michael A. Rosen, www.shaynew.com

p. 82: "Cruel Angel." Photograph © Jamie Griffiths

p. 83: Photograph © Jon Arensen

p. 85 top: Photograph © David Hancock/Skyscans

p. 85 bottom: Photograph by Todd Friedman © 1997 www.TFPhoto.com

p. 87 top: Photograph © Leni Riefenstahl

p. 87 bottom: Photograph © Rufus C. Camphausen

p. 88 top: Photograph © Angela Fisher

p. 88 bottom: Photograph © Carol Beckwith & Angela Fisher

p. 90 top: Photograph © Dominique Darbois

p. 90 bottom: Photograph © Rufus C. Camphausen

p. 91 top: Photograph © Stefan Richter 1997. All rights reserved.

p. 91 bottom: Photograph © Peter Bennetts

p. 92 top: Photograph © Charles Gatewood

p. 92 bottom: Photograph © Rufus C. Camphausen

p. 94: "Lovers." Photograph © Jamie Griffiths

p. 95: Twentieth-century miniature painting (Indra Sinha, *The Great Book of Tantra*, p. 79)

p. 98 top: Photograph © Don Snyder

p. 98 bottom: Photograph © Don Snyder

p. 104: Photograph courtesy of the Hutchinson Library

p. 105: Photograph © Christina Camphausen

p. 108: Photograph © Carol Beckwith & Angela Fisher

p. 109: Drawing from the German ethnography magazine *Globus*, vol. 30, 1876